ACKNOWLEDG

The single biggest contributor to my own growth has been Heather, my wife and business partner. Little did we know what a journey she got growing for us when she asked out this Mennonite farm boy for that first date on July 29, 1972! Not only have we grown ever closer since we married in 1977, but we've grown two businesses, a close and loving family, warm friends, financial security, spiritual meaning, and contributed to our community. It's been one heck of a journey so far. Visualization is a powerful magnetic force.

Thanks to our son Chris for brainstorming contributions on the WFL model at the center of this book, ongoing enthusiastic support, and technical help with organizing my extensive research notes. Thanks to our daughters Jenn and Vanessa for the strong love and support to our family and demonstrating how so many of the principles outlined here move us through adversity to "living, laughing and leading above the line." And thanks to all three of them for putting up with my Dad Jokes!

Scott Schweyer is a real professional — and all-around good guy — who continues to grow The CLEMMER Group's training and consulting capabilities and our Clients. Karen Lee has been a pivotal player in working with Scott to design and deliver outstanding and very practical training and culture-change programs. It's been a very rewarding and symbiotic partnership as we apply many of the concepts and approaches that have found their way into this book.

The CLEMMER Group support staff provides a strong backbone to our operations and allows me the time to focus on writing as they take care of business. Our Marketing Director, Aidan Crawford, continues to keep us on the forefront of technical communications by constantly improving our large and growing web site. He's also busy helping with my blog, monthly newsletter, *Improvement Points* (quotes from my articles e-mailed three times per week), monthly article service, press releases, digital e-mail blast, e-books, our affiliates program, opening new distribution channels, and lots of related work. Betty Kaita, Darlene Mashinter, Cara Tavares, and Gini Kechnie-Williams are not only highly effective in all their administrative support work, but they are delightful to work with. What a team!

For the past 20 years, Dave Chilton has been a good friend, an inspiration, and source of invaluable publishing advice (having sold over two million copies of *The Wealthy Barber,* he does seem to know a few things about the book business). This book benefitted greatly from the growing Chilton dynasty. Just as one door was closing for his sister, Susan, Dave opened the door that connected the two of us. Susan's strong editorial skills — and especially her headline-writing experience from her newspaper days — added powerful punch to the magazine-style format used

here. And we got another bonus with Bob Chilton (their father) applying his eagle-eyed proofreading skills to the final manuscript. Since both Susan and Bob originally helped Dave with his book, I can only hope a bit of the Chilton magic has rubbed off here!

I also owe big debts of gratitude to thousands of people who influenced my thinking or contributed to my own life experiences. I can't possibly list or thank them all individually. One major group consists of the many researchers, philosophers, authors, psychologists, and thought leaders referenced throughout this book. Another even larger group is comprised of the thousands of keynote, workshop, and retreat participants as well as readers I've worked or interacted with over the past few decades. Some of their experiences and perspectives are found in these pages. Many of their contributions, experiences, and applications underlie this book's concepts and approaches — especially the Tips and Techniques sections in Part Five.

Growing @ the Speed of Change

YOUR INSPIR-*ACTIONAL*
HOW-TO GUIDE FOR LEADING
YOURSELF AND OTHERS
THROUGH CONSTANT CHANGE

Library and Archives Canada Cataloguing in Publication

Clemmer, Jim, 1956-
    Growing @ the speed of change : your inspir-actional how-to guide for leading yourself and others through constant change / written by Jim Clemmer.

Includes bibliographical references and index.
ISBN 978-0-9813364-0-4

    1. Self-actualization (Psychology). 2. Inspiration. 3. Leadership.
I. Title. II. Title: Growing at the speed of change.

BF637.S4C5957 2009   158.1   C2009-905290-3

Published in 2009 by TCG Press,
an imprint of The CLEMMER Group Inc.

Design, layout, production: www.WeMakeBooks.ca
Printed and Bound in Canada

CONTENTS

When times get tough, the tough get growing.

GROWING FORWARD

"If you can keep your head when all about you are losing theirs, it's just possible you haven't grasped the situation."

Jean Kerr (1922–2003),
American author and playwright

The light dawned. I was in a meeting with my Achieve Group colleagues reviewing the rapid changes in our training and consulting business and sorting through our priorities for the coming quarter. We had doubled our already substantial business over the past 18 months. While the growth was exciting, it was also exhausting. We were piling on new programs, services, and organizational changes.

That was some time ago. I don't recall anything from the meeting except a rich conversation that ensued after I said, "Once we get through this crazy period and things settle down again…" I stopped myself. "Haven't we been saying that an awful lot lately?" I asked. Heads nodded around the room.

The descriptive phrase "hinge of history" coined by the futurist and writer Alvin Toffler sprang to mind. He presented strong evidence to show our world from the 1950s until roughly 2025 will be undergoing a seismic shift. Everything in our lives — business, politics, economics, the environment and our social structures — will change radically.

"I guess we — or at least I — have to get my head around the fact that this crazy period is normal and will be with us for many years to come," I reflected aloud. This led to an animated conversation. We needed a seismic shift in our thinking. The right approach was not to just plow through change, because a future period of stability is now a myth. Instead we agreed that we need to see constant, unpredictable, and tumultuous times as a normal and ongoing part of our company's life.

We need to thrive on and in our turbulent times.

As so often happens when you're newly attuned to an issue, not long after that meeting I came across a highly relevant remark. It was from Warren Bennis, Distinguished Professor of Business Administration and Founding Chairman of The Leadership Institute at the University of Southern California. (Ever since Warren said some very nice things about my book, *The Leader's Digest: Timeless Principles for Team and Organization Success,* I cite him and his wisdom whenever I can.)

Warren observed, "I can't recall a period of time that was as volatile, complex, ambiguous and tumultuous." He then quoted a top corporate leader of the day as observing, "If you're not confused, you don't know what's going on."[1] See: your confusion about our crazy, topsy-turvy times just shows you know what's going on!

Have you caught yourself

saying things like, "Once we get the new position filled... the restructuring is complete... the project is finished... the new software is installed... I get organized, things will settle down again?" Do things ever settle down? Of course not. And they never will in our lifetime.

THRIVING IN TURBULENT TIMES

"There is nothing stable in the world;
uproar's your only music."

John Keats (1795–1821), English poet. Letter, 13–19 Jan. 1818,
to his brothers George and Thomas Keats[2]

Turbulence means disorder, chaos, and instability. Turbulent times are unpredictable, disruptive, and confusing. Sound familiar? Yes. It sounds like life.

While it's tempting to want stability, predictability and orderliness, be very careful what you wish for. Writer, academic, journalist, and scholar of early modern English literature Germaine Greer warns, "Security is when everything is settled. When nothing can happen to you. Security is the denial of life."

Our greatest and most challenging turbulence comes with loss. That might include loss of a loved one, a job, health or mobility, a relationship, finances, certainty, or power and control. "Loss is nothing else but change, and change is Nature's delight," Emperor Augustus observed. Although we might like Nature to delight us more gently or less often, loss itself is neither good nor bad. It is what it is. How we deal with it determines whether it's good or bad. We can become bitter or better. Turbulence can be the hallmark of the best of times or the worst of times. The choice is yours.

To thrive on turbulence is to be vibrantly alive. To avoid turbulence is to wish life away. We must find ways to harness this powerful energy force for positive change throughout our personal and professional lives.

That's what *Growing @ the Speed of Change* is written to help you do.

WHAT'S NEW?
WRONG QUESTION.
WHAT MATTERS IS
WHAT WORKS

"Knowing is not enough; we must apply.
Willing is not enough; we must do."

Johann Wolfgang von Goethe (1749–1832), German writer

If you're looking for what's trendy or "new" in dealing with change, growth, or personal leadership, this is not the book for you. During my decades of work in this field I've seen many new approaches burst on the scene only to fade away. I have dozens of studies in my database library showing the high failure rates of these "hot" programs. What's most important when dealing with change and turbulence is not to be on the leading edge of thought or fashion, or spouting buzzwords and jargon that will be outdated within a few months. The key to effectiveness is simply implementing what works. And frankly, what works tends to be the tried, true, and proven. But even that only works if you put it into action.

When we built The Achieve Group during the eighties and early nineties, our slogan was "when theory is not enough." A core focus in our approach was "knowing isn't doing." We may know by doing, but we don't always do by knowing. Since The CLEMMER Group began in 1994, our focus has been on *practical* applications of timeless leadership principles for personal, team, and organizational success. I'm sorry, but there are no shortcuts or quick and easy solutions that require little effort or personal change. There is only the hard work of building basic habits. The CLEMMER Group focuses on applying proven techniques and approaches. That's what I've distilled for you in this book.

SHAPED BY OUR EXPERIENCE: WHERE I AM COMING FROM

"It is on your own self-knowledge and experience that the knowledge of everything else depends."

The Cloud of Unknowing, *a spiritual guidebook believed to have been written in the 14th century by an English monk*

An administrative assistant with no experience booking professional speakers was asked by her manager to call me about my availability and fee to deliver an opening keynote for their upcoming staff conference. When I gave her my fee, she replied, "For one hour….Wow! What a job! And you don't even have to have sex"! I didn't touch that one.

The fact is her company would really be paying for 30 years of study, experience, and practice summarized into one concentrated hour tailored to their needs. After the engagement, the admin assistant had a much better appreciation for the value I delivered to the audience in shifting perspectives on the roles everyone needs to play in leading at the speed of change. I certainly do feel very privileged to be well paid for my speaking, writing, consulting, facilitating, and training work.

I first experienced the transformational power of the personal growth and leadership principles that have since shaped my life and career — and form the key themes of this book — in a straight-commission sales job at Culligan Water Conditioning. I was 18. Applying these principles led to a fairly meteoric rise into supervisory, coaching, and training roles.

After participating in and helping to teach Dale Carnegie Training courses, I briefly joined that company to sell training and help deliver their public speaking, sales, and management courses. That was in 1977. Later that year — right after

Heather and I were married — Culligan rehired me as a sales trainer and internal consultant. During the next few years, I coached salespeople and owner/dealers using these principles and approaches. Sales rose dramatically. At age 24, I was promoted to General Manager of Culligan Canada's largest branch in Edmonton, Alberta. Again, these principles had a dramatic impact on the staff I was leading. During my 18 months in that position we increased revenues 35 percent.

In 1981, I left Culligan to colead The Achieve Group, a management training and consulting company started in Edmonton by Art McNeil. Shortly after that, Heather and I moved back to Southern Ontario and worked together to build Achieve's Client base (we've always capitalized the most important people to our business) and start our family. Working with California-based training designer Zenger Miller throughout the 1980s, I hired and trained dozens of Achieve account executives, trainers, consultants, and support staff. We not only sold programs and services teaching these personal, team, and organization effectiveness principles; we also built our own company around them. By 1990, The Achieve Group had become Canada's largest training and consulting company.

In 1991, Achieve was purchased by Times Mirror and merged with Zenger Miller, Learning International, and Kaset to form AchieveGlobal. For the next few years, I was an executive team facilitator and coach traveling extensively across Canada and the U.S. I delivered keynote presentations and facilitated dozens of senior management team retreats and coaching sessions. Some of our Clients hired us because my new book, *Firing on All Cylinders: The Service/Quality System for High-Powered Corporate Performance,* was a top seller and caught the Total Quality Management wave (later this evolved to Lean Six Sigma techniques). The unsuccessful ones were jumping on a fad bandwagon and seeing limited results from their limited efforts. But most of our Clients diligently applied the team and organization principles and saw dramatic performance results — as well as greater personal success.

In 1994, Heather and I founded The CLEMMER Group. Building upon my third book, *Pathways to Performance: A Guide to Transforming Yourself, Your Team, and Your Organization*, I and a few associates started with a small number of customized workshops, keynote presentations, management retreats, consulting, coaching, and training programs. Our experiences and offerings have expanded exponentially with new books and related application guides and training materials.

My next book, *Growing the Distance: Timeless Principles for Personal, Career, and Family Success*, became one of my most popular because of its broader application, unique "browser's digest" format, and inspirational messages. With that book, I developed our Timeless Leadership Principles *"Leadership Wheel"* model that also formed the central structure of its companion book, *The Leader's Digest: Timeless Principles for Team and Organization Success*. This model for leading ourselves and others became a central structure of The CLEMMER Group's leadership development workshops and training materials.

For my next book, I studied the craft of storytelling through novels. *Moose on the Table®: A Novel Approach to Communications @ Work* was an "edutaining case study," or work of fiction focused on Pete Leonard, a struggling manager. Pete's story brought to life the core personal growth, leadership development, and organizational effectiveness principles detailed in my previous books.

You can get more background on my books, materials, workshops, and The CLEMMER Group consulting and training services, view dozens of video clips of me presenting many of these principles, and read through over 300 articles, on our web site at *www.Jim Clemmer.com*.

ALL ABOARD FOR
THE CITY TOUR

"Books are the compasses and telescopes and sextants and charts which others have prepared to help us navigate the dangerous seas of human life."

Jesse Lee Bennett (1885–1931), American author

Heather and I love to travel. A great perk of my work is that I am invited to speak or lead workshops and retreats in some beautiful places around the world. Heather carefully selects which ones she joins me for. When we travel to a new city, we start our stay with a city tour. This gives us a broad overview of the area and helps us decide where we want to spend more time.

Growing @ the Speed of Change is like a city tour. It's a broad overview of proven core principles for dealing with change, turbulence, and personal growth at home and at work. Here I offer you the keys that will unlock a happy and successful life. As you read or browse through *Growing @ the Speed of Change*, you'll be able

to jump off the bus, take a quick look around, snap a few photos, and then reboard for the next destination.

We could spend a lot more time at each stop in this book. I really had to work at condensing each chapter to its bare essence. After all, it's encapsulating my books, workbooks full of dozens of assessments and exercises, hundreds of how-to action points, a monthly *newsletter* begun in 2003, and my *blog*. Yikes! So at the end of each chapter I have added a "To Keep You Growing" section to guide you to my other writings for more in-depth study, additional examples, further inspiration, and practical applications.

If you're a reader of my *books*, *blog*, or *newsletters*, you'll find *Growing @ the Speed of*

Change complements and refreshes my core themes and approaches. If you are new to my writing, welcome aboard. Prepare to start *Growing @ the Speed of Change*.

WHAT SETS THIS BOOK APART

"Thousands of grapes are pressed to fill one jar with wine, and the grape skin and pulp are tossed to the birds. So it is with these grapes of wisdom from the ages. Much has been filtered and tossed to the wind. Only the pure truth lies distilled in the words to come."[3]

Og Mandino (1923–1996), *The Greatest Salesman in the World*

Some people like to build things with their hands. As Heather can attest, I was not blessed with the handyman gene. My farmer father and my cabinet-maker brother kept that gene to themselves. I like to build with words. My grandmother was a published poet in Elmira, Ontario, so it's likely her set of genes that made me handier with a keyboard than with a hammer. (That's not to say there aren't times when I would like to use a hammer on the keyboard!)

Growing @ the Speed of Change is the culmination of over three decades of my study, personal application, and ongoing research and writing. This book also captures my coaching and training of thousands of consulting Clients and workshop participants who are dealing with tough changes and adversity. *Growing @ the Speed of Change* also draws from evolving research from emerging fields such as quantum mechanics, consciousness, cognitive/positive psychology, happiness, and emotional intelligence.

With many quotations used throughout this book, I have

shown birth/death dates of the author to set the observation in the context of its time. In many cases, older comments show just how timeless these issues really are, as we rediscover and reapply them to our lives today. Dates for books and printed or published articles can be found in the endnotes citing the source.

Growing @ the Speed of Change builds upon many of the personal growth and self-leadership concepts I first introduced in *Growing the Distance: Timeless Principles for Personal, Career, and Family Success*. As with *Growing the Distance*, I've added inspirational stories, personal and Client examples, fables, and humor to enliven and simplify what can be dry research or complex concepts. But what's especially exciting and different about *Growing @ the Speed of Change* are the hundreds of practical action ideas I've added. I've attempted to make this book "inspir-actional."

"Inspir-*actional*?" No, it's not a typo. I'm aiming to inspire you, then give you the plans you need to take action. Those are

the two main sections — and objectives — of this book.

Here are some other features I hope you'll find make this book unique and a treasured addition to your library:

- "Browser's digest" or magazine-style format with three main streams:
  - Short sections of easily digested commentary, observations, and advice.
  - Condensed sidebars with stories, fables, "wise words," or how-to points.
  - Classical or modern quotations summarizing or underscoring the key message of the section or sidebar.
- "Edutaining" conversational style with liberal doses of humor and personal stories.
- Dozens of how-to practical applications to move you from inspiration to application.
- "To Keep You Growing" section at the end of each chapter links to dozens of my articles, books, workbooks, or web site sections so you can dig deeper.
- Over 150 endnotes of all quotations, studies, and

references that can be used for further study.

These are all approaches designed to make *Growing @ The Speed of Change* a quick read, for our fast-moving society. Whether you keep this book in a boardroom or a bathroom, I hope you keep it close at hand and that any page you flip to will offer you a practical quick hit. Wherever you skim it, you'll be "flush" with success. Which leads us to….

WIT HAPPENS

"Don't take life too seriously. You're never going to get out of it alive anyway."

Herb True, *author of* Humor Power: How to Get It, Give It and Gain (1980)

Here's where my kids would jump in with a warning about my Dad Jokes. When Chris, Jenn, and Vanessa were teenagers and dating, they'd warn new boyfriends or girlfriends not to laugh at my wisecracks. "Don't encourage him," they'd caution, as I tried to stamp a HELLO! My Name Is sticker on the new visitor's jacket. There really was quite a parade of them.

In my workshops and retreats I often kid about kidding and pledge to go easy on the Dad Jokes. After one session, a participant — a fellow Dad Joker — e-mailed me: "We have three children as well. They too groan at 'Dad Jokes.' In fact, a couple of years ago they and my wife implemented a house rule of only allowing me two Dad Jokes a night! Great stuff...keep it coming...and don't give up the Dad jokes."

I am assuming you, dear reader, are not on a humor-reduced diet. A sense of humor is critical in dealing with the nasty changes and dangerous turbulence that can violently shake our comfortable lives. If we take it all too seriously, it can scare the wit out of us.

www.JimClemmer.com

- See the "Jim Clemmer" section of our web site at http://www.jimclemmer.com/jim. You can read more about my background, interviews, and The CLEMMER Group's core models and frameworks.
- The Media Center at http://www.jimclemmer.com/media has a series of TV interviews and a Frequently Asked Questions – and Answers – section on my background and perspectives.

Books

- "Introduction" of *Pathways to Performance: A Guide to Transforming Yourself, Your Team, and Your Organization.* The book's Introduction is available as a free download from our web site at http://www.jimclemmer.com/pathways.
- "Introduction" of *Growing the Distance: Timeless Principles for Personal, Career, and Family Success.* The book's Introduction is available as a free download from our web site at http://www.jimclemmer.com/gtd.

PART
ONE

Shift
Happens

I

CHANGE:
You pay your taxes.
You can even preplan your funeral.
But how you deal with the third certainty in life
will make or break you.

WINDS OF CHANGE: LIFE BLOWS ON

"There is nothing constant in the universe; All ebb and flow, and every shape that's born; Bears in its womb the seeds of change."

Ovid, 1st century Roman poet

The world is unpredictable, turbulent, and chaotic. Nature eschews stability, predictability, and sameness. The seasons of life follow eternally repeating patterns of birth, growth, decline, and death. That makes room for renewal and another cycle to begin. Often the cycles don't play out in a stable or orderly way. We may see bursts of growth that lead us to feel as if abundance and expansion will go on forever. Surely the trees will grow to the sky.

Then when we least expect it, a storm springs up and instantly destroys what had taken years to grow and develop. This often creates different conditions that require something fresh and adaptive to fill the void. A new species might emerge. A new skill set might develop. A radically different approach might appear. A totally new opportunity will open up. This is creative destruction. This is evolution. This is life.

This cycle of change may vary in its timing and intensity, but that the cycle is recurring never changes. Heraclitus was a philosopher living in ancient Greece around 500 BC. His greatest legacy is his doctrine that perpetual change is central to the universe. Predating and influencing Plato, Socrates, and Aristotle, Heraclitus made a series of observations on the unchanging nature of change. These centuries-old truths are highly relevant for us today:

These centuries-old truths are highly relevant for us today.

"Nothing endures but change."

"You could not step twice into the same river; for other waters are ever flowing on to you."

"All is flux, nothing stays still."

"There is nothing permanent except change."

Permanent Impermanence: Unchanging Cycles of Change

"Life is a series of natural and spontaneous changes. Don't resist them — that only creates sorrow. Let reality be reality."

> Lao-tse, 6th century BC
> Chinese philosopher

Julia was exhausted. Business was outstanding. Her team was scrambling to keep up and she was stretched thin. They had trouble finding enough good people to fill the new positions that were being created by the company's rapid growth.

During a family gathering she talked about her crazy-busy life and shared her frustration with a favorite uncle who was semiretired from decades of building successful businesses. Uncle Vern had become a mentor and great sounding board for Julia. He smiled knowingly as she outlined her growth problems at work. As they talked, Uncle Vern gave Julia nuggets of sage advice from his years of accumulated wisdom. The comment that she puzzled over most during the following weeks was "This too will pass."

Julia was exhausted. Revenues had plunged off a cliff. In a few short months their high-growth market sharply reversed direction at a dizzying rate. Their company was scrambling to cut costs and began laying people off. She was stretched thin trying to cover vacant positions on her team. All the while Julia grew increasingly insecure about her own job.

During another family gathering Julia anxiously sought out Uncle Vern's advice. He told her of similar market downturns he'd lived through and the sleepless nights he'd experienced as his life work and life savings hung in the balance. She took comfort in much of his wise counsel on the way home that evening. The comment that stayed with her over the coming weeks was "This too will pass."

THE CHANGE PARADOX: DÉJÀ VU ALL OVER AGAIN

"How wonderful that we have met with a paradox.
Now we have some hope of making progress."

Niels Bohr (1885–1962), Danish Nobel
prize-winning physicist who made fundamental
contributions to understanding atomic
structure and quantum mechanics

Imagine being a time traveler and taking a "magical history tour" of the vast array of significant and small "hinges of history," or pivotal changes throughout the world's major cultures in the past three thousand years. After just a few dozen stops, you'd start to see and hear recurring themes: "All this change is happening too fast"; "Things were much better in the good old days"; "Let's destroy this new technology that's spoiling our life"; "Nobody wants to work anymore"; "Stop the world, I want to get off," and many similar refrains.

You could drop in to the Forum in ancient Rome and listen to renowned statesman, orator, and writer Marcus Tullius Cicero around the time of Julius Caesar. You might feel his pain as he laments, "Times are bad. Children no longer obey their parents, and everyone is writing a book." Or you could sit in on the County Council meeting of 1904 in London, Ontario as councilors voted to petition the provincial legislature to regulate automobiles in the country. Why? They argued that the "automobile is a curse"[4] due to the frightening of horses.

People frightened by change often demonize the new and mythologize the old. Let's pretend you could continue time traveling and now move forward through time, swinging from one hinge of history to another, like a monkey through the jungle treetops. You'd likely be vigorously nodding your head in the 19th century when reformer, politician, and newspaper editor Horace Greely observes,

> **"In every age, 'the good old days' were a myth."**
> Brooks Atkinson

"The illusion that times that were are better than those that are, has probably pervaded all ages." As you move into the middle of the 20th century, you would be numbed from hearing the same messages over and over again. And you'd be agreeing with *New York Times* theater critic Brooks Atkinson, "In every age 'the good old days' were a myth. No one ever thought they were good at the time. For every age has consisted of crises that seemed intolerable to the people who lived through them."[5]

Back to the Future: Same Change, Different Century

"What if globalization is not a new trend, but a return to a pattern of life that dates back more than a dozen centuries, shaping the world long before computers, before mass media, before capitalism... this new school of thought — dubbed 'archaic globalization' by some practitioners — is about to transform our understanding of the last thousand years, now that several of its adherents have published important large-scale studies that have begun to revolutionize entire fields of history."[6]

"When did our lives go global? Try 300 AD" by Doug Saunders, The Globe & Mail

"Contrary to what most everybody believes, however, this transition period is remarkably similar to the two transition periods that preceded it during the nineteenth century: the one in the 1830s and 1840s, following the invention of railroads, postal services, telegraph, photography, limited-liability business, and investment banking; and the second one, in the 1870s and 1880s, following the invention of steel making; electric light and electric power; synthetic organic chemicals, sewing machines and washing machines; central heating; the subway; the elevator and with it apartment and office buildings and skyscrapers; the telephone and typewriter and with them the modern office; the business corporation and commercial banking."[7]

Peter Drucker (1909–2005), author of 39 books and hundreds of articles on leadership, management, and organization effectiveness, widely considered to be the father of "modern management"

"These social and economic changes… were uneven and unsettling. They opened up differentials between groups and between different societies. They spawned lust for wealth, envy, and distrust of neighbors. They led to overseas wars, unequal taxation, social turmoil, and the questioning of established authority, royal and religious. The turmoil was worldwide."[8]

A description of 1780 by C.A. Bayly (1945–) Cambridge University historian and author of a historical study on globalization, The Birth of the Modern World

"In times like these, it is helpful to remember that there have always been times like these."

Paul Harvey (1918–2009), American radio commentator

BLOWING OR GROWING IN THE WINDS OF CHANGE

"Yesterday's home run won't win tomorrow's ballgames."

Babe Ruth (1895–1948), legendary baseball player, also known as "The Sultan of Swat" and "The Home Run King"

There's plenty of evidence to show that we're in the midst of yet another major world shift. We're living through another of dozens in a centuries-long line of disruptive pivot points. Part of nature's rejuvenation is a phase of cleansing and purging. This usually rocks our current frameworks, expectations, and maybe too-comfortable lifestyles. Cleansing and purging makes room for the new order.

Depending on our perspective, a hinge of history such as we're currently experiencing is either an invigorating or a cursed time to be alive. If you choose to thrive on turbulence and change, this time is a rare gift to participate in, and help shape, new ways of doing and being in our personal lives, organizations, communities, and societies. Years from now, we will look at this hinge of history as an era of upheaval and renewal that inspired us to a higher and different order of prosperity. If we continue history's long trends, we're moving toward a great renaissance of spirit, cooperation, love, redefined wealth, and care for the earth's environment.

During our workshops — team-planning sessions in

particular — we often compile a list of major trends rocking our world. And it is a long, long list: technology, customer expectations, competition, globalization, business/organizational models, product or service response or development times, workforce demographics and cultural diversity, government regulations and policies, employee attitudes and expectations in the workplace, environmental issues and concerns, and economic gyrations between rapid expansion and sharp contraction…

I could go on, but you get the picture: these are all things shaping us or within our power to shape. This is an invigorating and great time — or a threatening and disastrous time — to be alive.

Head Winds: Accelerating Corporate Turbulence

"An analysis of Fortune 1000 corporations shows that between 1973 and 1983, 35 percent of the companies in the top twenty were new. The number of new companies increases to 45 percent when the comparison is between 1983 and 1993. It increases even further, to 60 percent, when the comparison is between 1993 and 2003."[9]

> *Edward E. Lawler III and Christopher G. Worley,* Built to Change: How to Achieve Sustained Organizational Effectiveness

"Although the Fortune 100 comprises the most stable corporations in the world, there has been considerable churn in the list. Only 26% of the companies on it in 1980 were still there in 2001."[10]

> *"The New Road to the Top," Peter Cappelli and Monika Hamori*

"Even perennially successful companies are finding it more difficult to deliver consistently superior returns. In their 1994 best-seller Built to Last, Jim Collins and Jerry Porras singled out 18 'visionary' companies that had consistently outperformed their peers between 1950 and 1990. But over the last ten years, just six of these companies managed to outperform the Dow Jones Industrial Average. The other twelve — a group that includes companies like Disney, Motorola, Ford, Nordstrom, Sony, and Hewlett-Packard — have apparently gone from great to merely OK. Any way you cut it, success has never been so fragile."[11]

> *"The Quest for Resilience," Gary Hamel and Liisa Välikangas*

I PREDICT... MORE UNPREDICTABILITY

"There are two classes of people who tell what is going to happen in the future: Those who don't know, and those who don't know they don't know."

John Kenneth Galbraith (1908–2006), Canadian-American economist, Harvard professor, advisor to U.S. presidents, and author of over four dozen books and one thousand papers

It's as predictable as champagne and the ball drop in Times Square on New Year's Eve. In late December and early January, futurists, forecasters, and analysts line up with the seers, fortune tellers, and clairvoyants to prophesize what the coming year has in store for us. Instead of tea leaves, animal entrails, and crystal balls, the "experts" will be using data, charts, and complex theories. And they'll be wrong.

Since the dawn of time, part of us has wanted to know what the future has in store. Another part of us realizes that if we knew precisely what surprises lie ahead or what unavoidable crisis was going to hit us, we'd be so filled with anticipation or doom, we wouldn't live in the present and enjoy the moment now.

An extensive study of this popular topic is outlined in *The Fortune Sellers: The Big Business of Buying and Selling Predictions.* The author, William Sherden, studied the dismal history — and multibillion-dollar industry — of forecasting. (He calls it the second oldest profession.) Sherden concludes "of these sixteen types of forecast, only two — one-day-ahead weather forecasts and the aging of the population — can be counted on; the rest are about as reliable as the fifty-fifty odds in flipping a coin. And only one of the sixteen — short-term weather forecasts — has any scientific foundation."[12]

I, too, keep an extensive database of failed predictions. I have collected hundreds of examples and dozens of studies showing the woeful record of forecasting. Some of my all-time favorites are included here. When I hear an economist or any other forecaster making predictions, a voice in my head says, "Yeah, right! You have no idea what's going to happen." These ponderous forecasters remind me of a banner my cousin had hanging on the wall in his bedroom when we were kids: "If you're so smart, why aren't you rich?"

Why are these self-proclaimed "experts" working for someone else or just appearing as talking heads on news networks? If they're so prescient, why aren't they multibillionaires running the most successful businesses or investment funds on earth? Or if they're altruistic, why aren't they directing humanitarian organizations in preparation for impending famines, wars, and natural disasters?

The great British Prime Minister Winston Churchill, who led England during the Second World War, wryly reflected on his frustration in getting "expert" advice: "It's the ability to foretell what will happen tomorrow, next month and next year — and to explain afterwards why it did not happen." British actor and writer Peter Ustinov echoes, "If the world should blow itself up, the last audible voice would be that of an expert saying it can't be done."

A couple goes to a fair, where there's a large, impressive-looking machine. The husband puts in a coin and receives a card telling him his age and what kind of person he is. He reads it and gets excited. It says: "You're brilliant and charming. Women fall all over you." His wife grabs the card from him and turns it over. "Aha!" she crows, "they got your age wrong, too."

Seer Madness: False Prophets and Experts of Error

"University of California political psychologist Philip Tetlock spent two decades asking foreign policy experts to make predictions about world events, and then tracking their accuracy. In that time, he has assembled a database of more than 80,000 individual predictions by 284 experts. The result: Expertise and experience made very little difference (he published his findings in his book, Expert Political Judgment). Experts on the whole barely outperform a coin toss in predicting the future…. The best experts…can get their success rate up to nearly 60 percent — better than 'heads or tails,' but not by much."[13]

"A talk with Philip Tetlock: Expertise is overrated," Rick Heller, The Boston Globe

"You have been a world-class sap for years. Why? For listening to the economic and political forecasts of experts. We in the media have been irresponsible fools for reporting those forecasts. And the experts themselves? Delusional egomaniacs — and maybe even con artists… Experts can also give far more reasons for their predictions than non-experts can. Their vast erudition lets them explain at daunting length why something will or won't happen. Not that all those reasons make the forecasts one bit better."[14]

"Ditch the 'Experts': Grading pundits and prognosticators: More famous = less accurate," Geoffrey Colvin, Fortune

"The accuracy of an expert's predictions actually has an inverse relationship to his or her self-confidence, renown, and, beyond a certain point, depth of knowledge. People who follow current events by reading the papers and news-magazines regularly can guess what is likely to happen about as accurately as the specialists whom the papers quote. Our system of expertise is completely inside out: it rewards bad judgments over good ones."

"Everybody's An Expert: Putting predictions to the test," Louis Menand, The New Yorker[15]

"Trouble is, despite their efforts, forecasters aren't particularly accurate and their track record isn't improving, particularly when it comes to predicting recessions. 'They tend to make the same forecasting mistakes,' said Merv Daub, professor emeritus at Queen's University's business school. 'Much of the process relies on guessing what will happen to external factors such as the global economic and political environment,' said Daub, who has extensively researched the accuracy of forecasting. 'How the hell do you forecast these things?' he said. 'Forecasters are not witches. They don't possess some mythical way of foreseeing the future.'"[16]

"The Prophets of Profit," Steven Theobald reporting on The Toronto Star's analysis of 20 years of mostly inaccurate annual forecasts

"Victor Zarnowitz, a professor at the University of Chicago and one of the leading trackers of economic forecasting accuracy, analyzed the error rates for six prominent economic forecasters — the big three plus GE, the Bureau of Economic Analysis, and the National Bureau of Economic Research — in predicting real gross national product (GNP) growth and inflation... He found that of the forty-eight predictions made by the economists, forty-six missed the turning points in the economy... Roy A. Batchelor and Pami Dua, professors at City University in London and the University of Connecticut, respectively... In analyzing the track records of thirty-two forecasters, they found almost no differences in forecast accuracy among the different economic schools of thought... The Economist was right to declare that economic forecasters 'are worse than useless: they can do actual long-term damage to the economy.'"[17]

The Fortune Sellers: The Big Business of Buying and Selling Predictions, William A. Sherden

Forecast Bombast: The (Un)foreseeable Future

"I have traveled the length and breadth of this country and talked with the best people, and I can assure you that data processing is a fad that won't last out the year."

The editor in charge of business books for Prentice Hall in 1957

"There is no reason anyone would want a computer in their home."

Ken Olson in 1977 when he was president and founder of Digital Equipment Corp — a pioneering computer company that no longer exists

"In 1960 the Beatles got an audition with one of England's top promoters. They failed."[18]

The Beatles: 40th Anniversary Collectors Edition

"Rail travel at high speeds is not possible because passengers, unable to breathe, would die of asphyxia."

Dionysius Lardner, Professor of Natural Philosophy and Astronomy at University College, London, and author of The Steam Engine Explained and Illustrated *(1830)*

"Stock prices have reached what looks like a permanently high plateau."

Irving Fisher (1867–1947), Professor of Economics at Yale University, a few days before the stock market crash in October of 1929

"The abdomen, the chest, and the brain will forever be shut from the intrusion of the wise and humane surgeon."

Sir John Eric Ericksen, British surgeon, appointed Surgeon-Extraordinary to Queen Victoria in 1873

"X-rays will prove to be a hoax.... No balloon and no aero plane will ever be practically successful... There is nothing new to be discovered in physics now. All that remains is more and more precise measurement."

William Thomson, 1st Baron Kelvin (or Lord Kelvin), late 19th century British mathematical physicist and engineer

"So many centuries after the Creation it is unlikely that anyone could find hitherto unknown lands of any value."

1486 committee advising King Ferdinand and Queen Isabella of Spain regarding a proposal by Christopher Columbus, six years before he discovered the Americas

"There is not the slightest indication that nuclear energy will ever be obtainable. It would mean that the atom would have to be shattered at will."

Albert Einstein (1879–1955), Nobel Prize-winning theoretical physicist

"The (Atomic) bomb will never go off, and I speak as an expert in explosives."

Fleet Admiral William Daniel Leahy to President Truman in 1944

*Mayhem, madness and miracles:
life is out of our control. Our reaction
to it, though, is not.*

LIFE ISN'T FAIR

*"If life was fair, Elvis would be alive and
all the impersonators would be dead."*
Johnny Carson (1925–2005), American comedian
and former host of The Tonight Show

Life isn't fair. The world is full of injustice and inequality. Billions live in horrible poverty. Brutal wars kill and maim millions of blameless people. Corrupt governments destroy entire countries' quality of life. Business leaders bilk thousands of average investors out of their life savings and drive economies into ruin, throwing people out of work around the world. Diseases bring devastating disabilities or death to innocent children. Genetic illnesses cripple or dramatically shorten the lives of even those with the healthiest of lifestyles. Pandemics infect the globe, cutting down young and old alike. Drunk drivers kill parents, kids, brothers, sisters, spouses, friends or themselves. Mental illness strikes individuals and families in random patterns. Alcoholism takes hold and wreaks havoc in the lives of some "party-hearty drinkers" and not others. Natural disasters destroy one community or area while sparing others. Entire races are excluded, murdered, or lose limbs because of their skin pigmentation.

∞

Life isn't fair. The world is full of miracles and narrow escapes. A fierce tornado destroys two homes completely but one home right between them is untouched. A car careens out of control, flips, rolls, misses two trees, comes to rest on its roof, and the unbelted passengers walk away uninjured. A tiny minority of the world's population enjoys a vast majority of its wealth simply because of the country, family, or time they were born in. A heavy smoker lives a healthy life into his or her nineties and dies peacefully during sleep. An average, dependable employee shows up for work every day at a start-up company that grows a thousandfold; he or she gets a few stock options, and becomes incredibly wealthy. An entire generation is presented with economic growth and vast job options. People with the same skin color, gender, and ethnicity as those in power are promoted. Some people have natural immunity to lethal diseases that strike many around them. A careless and inattentive driver enjoys decades of crash-free cruising. Hundreds of millions are born with sound minds and healthy bodies to loving and nurturing parents in peaceful countries. Countless millions have an abundance of consumer goods, shelter, clean water, and healthy food available.

∞

Life is turbulent, life is impermanent, life is constant change, life is unpredictable, and life is unfair. All of these are life's external conditions that each of us inherits the day we're born. Life is life. Life is what it is. Whether these outer conditions are good or bad, positive or negative, or make us happy or unhappy depends on our inner conditions. It's up to us.

Think about lucky and unlucky people you know. Don't the "lucky" people adapt better, bounce back from tragedy or adversity more quickly, learn from change, whether good or bad, and deal with things in a way you admire? We might ask ourselves, "How do they do that?" As we'll see in the pages ahead, we can all learn to do it.

We may be getting an incredibly turbulent ride in this life or we might be coasting along smoothly. We may not choose what life throws at us. But we do choose how we respond. Life gives us the power to create our own reality.

THRIVE ON TURBULENCE BY GROWING FOR IT

*"Our wealth, health, and very existence
are all extremely provisional. Here today and
gone tomorrow. This is the way the world is
and the way it always will be."*[19]

*Punnadhammo Bhikkhu (1944–), ordained Theravadan
Buddhist monk and abbot of the Arrow River Forest Hermitage,
a Buddhist forest monastery near Thunder Bay, Ontario*

Mystics, philosophers, and spiritual teachers have for centuries emphasized that a fundamental key to dealing with life's turbulence is acceptance of life's impermanence. We're here today and gone tomorrow — making room for the next cycle of renewal. In their book *The Art of Happiness: A Handbook for Living,* the Dalai Lama and Howard Cutler describe a central tenet of Buddhism critical to thriving in tumultuous times:

"Without cultivating a pliant mind, our outlook becomes brittle and our relationship to the world becomes characterized by fear. But by adopting a flexible, malleable approach to life, we can maintain our composure even in the most restless and turbulent conditions. It is through our efforts to achieve a flexible mind that we can nurture the resiliency of the human spirit."[20]

Unpredictable, unexpected, rapid, and yes, unfair change

rocks governments, businesses, and people worldwide. And will keep on doing so. There's no "getting through this crazy period" to some mythical place of stability, or predictable sameness. Whether these changes are deadly threats or growth opportunities often depends upon how they are dealt with. When our rate of growth and learning is slow or stalled, any change can be sudden and overwhelming. It leaves us scrambling to catch up with its impact, learning, or skills we need to just cope — never mind thrive.

In their book, *Built to Change: How to Achieve Sustained Organizational Effectiveness*, Professor Edward Lawler III and research scientist Christopher Worley of the University of Southern California's Center for Effective Organizations write, "Organizations that are built to change must view people as open and willing to learn and as eager to try new things. They must have structures that are constantly refocusing attention and resources on both current and future problems and opportunities. They must have reward systems that encourage learning and growth as well as current value-added activities. Finally, they must have financial processes and other systems that support innovation and the start-up of new products and services."[21]

The Curious Case of Life's Unfairness

"The most unfair thing about life is the way it ends. I mean, life is tough. It takes up a lot of your time. What do you get at the end of it? A death. What's that, a bonus? I think the life cycle is all backwards. You should die first, get it out of the way. Then you live in an old age home. You get kicked out when you're too young, you get a gold watch, you go to work. You work forty years until you're young enough to enjoy your retirement. You do drugs, alcohol, you party, and you get ready for high school. You go to grade school, you become a kid, you play, you have no responsibilities, you become a little baby, you go back into the womb, you spend your last nine months floating... you finish off as an orgasm."

George Carlin (1937–2008), American comedian, actor, author, and winner of five Grammy Awards for comedy albums

Wise Words: Growing for a Change

"Jolts of correction appear more menacing than downward drift."

Jane Jacobs (1916–2006), American-born Canadian writer and activist

"It's not so much that we're afraid of change or so in love with the old ways, but it's that place in between that we fear... It's like being between trapezes. It's Linus when his blanket is in the dryer. There's nothing to hold on to."

Marilyn Ferguson (1938–2008), American author, editor, and speaker, best known for her book The Aquarian Conspiracy: Personal and Social Transformation in Our Time

"The only thing that one really knows about human nature is that it changes. Change is the one quality we can predicate of it. The systems that fail are those that rely on the permanency of human nature, and not on its growth and development."[22]

Oscar Wilde (1854–1900), Irish playwright, poet, and novelist

"If we don't change, we don't grow. If we don't grow, we aren't actually living."[23]

Gail Sheehy (1937–), American writer and speaker on our life cycles or "passages"

"Too much security and the refusal to evolve, to embrace change, leads to a kind of death."[24]

Jean Vanier, Becoming Human (1998)

TO KEEP YOU GROWING

Here's where you can find more of my material on the topics covered in this chapter.

www.JimClemmer.com

- A selection of articles on Change Management at http://www.jimclemmer.com/change.
- Short items, reader comments, and observations from past issues of *The Leader Letter* (my monthly newsletter) on Change Management at http://www.jimclemmer.com/newsletter/?cat=16.
- Peruse a few dozen articles on Personal Growth and Continuous Improvement at http://www.jimclemmer.com/growth.
- A selection of my writing and reader discussions on Personal Growth and Continuous Improvement from my

blog and **monthly newsletter** at http://www.jimclemmer.com/newsletter/?cat=15.

Books

- Chapter One, "Changing, Learning, and Improving" of *Pathways to Performance: A Guide to Transforming Yourself, Your Team, and Your Organization*. Chapter One is available as a free download.
- Chapter One, "The Way of the Leader" of *Growing the Distance: Timeless Principles for Personal, Career, and Family Success*. Chapter One is available as a free download.

PART TWO

The "Real" of Life

II

Warning!!
This chapter could really change your reality.

REALITY CHECK

"Reality is what we take to be true. What we take to be true is what we believe. What we believe is based upon our perceptions. What we perceive depends upon what we look for. What we look for depends upon what we think. What we think depends upon what we perceive. What we perceive determines what we believe. What we believe determines what we take to be true. What we take to be true is our reality."[25]

Gary Zukav, The Dancing Wu Li Masters:
An Overview of the New Physics (2001)

"Get real!" "You're not living in the real world." "That's a pipe dream that's completely out of touch with reality!" "Your delusional flights of fancy sound good but in actual fact…" "The reality of our situation is…" "Let me give you a dose of reality."

Anyone trying to stay positive and navigate turbulent times is faced with responses such as these. But what is reality? Is there such a thing as objective reality? Our understanding of "the real world" is evershifting and extremely perplexing. The nature of reality is at the heart of fierce philosophical, spiritual, and psychological debates that have raged for thousands of years. The early 20th century Italian playwright Luigi Pirandello captures the elusive concept we're dealing with: "Whatever is a reality today, whatever you touch and believe in and that seems real for you today, is going to be — like the reality of yesterday — an illusion tomorrow." One of his surrealistic American plays,

> **"Reality leaves a lot to the imagination."**
> John Lennon (1940–1980), English songwriter, musician, and founding member of The Beatles

1927's *Right You Are (If You Think You Are)*, dealt with another age-old debate in the same realm as reality: the nature of truth.

There is a vast variety of today's "facts of life" that were once considered illusory and are now accepted as reality. French Emperor Napoleon Bonaparte's dismissal of American engineer Robert Fulton's steamboat is a good example: "What, sir, would you make a ship sail against the wind and currents by lighting a bonfire under her deck? I pray you excuse me. I have no time to listen to such nonsense."

No doubt Bonaparte and other "experts" of his day told Fulton to get his head out of the clouds and "live in the real world." A 1921 *New York Times* editorial about Robert Goddard's revolutionary rocket work tried to bring him "back to reality" with what were at the time known to be irrefutable scientific "facts": "Professor Goddard does not know the relation between action and reaction and the need to have something better than a vacuum against which to react. He seems to lack the basic knowledge ladled out daily in high schools."

Imagine European time-traveling engineers or scientists from around 1400 looking at our life today. How dramatically would their view of reality shift when they saw this round (not flat) earth from the moon? Imagine the array of "facts" they'd have to radically and completely alter when they saw how we travel, communicate, grow our food, treat our illnesses, light and heat our homes, or entertain ourselves. How would they return to their time and try to define reality to their 13th century contemporaries? They'd be burned at the stake for heresy or locked away as raving lunatics.

What about 600 years from now? Given how rapidly the fields of science, technology, psychology, and sociology alone are evolving, today's "reality" will undoubtedly have altered even more dramatically in the next 600 years than in the last 600. We can't even imagine what radical new "reality" will be accepted as facts of life in the 27th century. By today's understanding of how our world works, they would seem utterly impossible and absolutely unbelievable. Just like Fulton's foolish steamboat.

The Slippery Subjectivity of Reality

"Reality: *(noun) all of your experiences that determine how things appear to you; 'his world was shattered'; 'we live in different worlds'; 'for them demons were as much a part of reality as trees were.'"*[26]

> From WordNet lexical database of English, Cognitive Science Laboratory, Princeton University

"Given that external reality is a fiction, the writer's role is almost superfluous. He does not need to invent the fiction because it is already there."[27]

> J.G. Ballard (1930–2009), a British writer who spent four years of his childhood in a Japanese prison camp, an experience described in his 1984 book Empire of the Sun

"There are intangible realities which float near us, formless and without words; realities which no one has thought out, and which are excluded for lack of interpreters."[28]

> Natalie Clifford Barney (1876–1972), American expatriate who lived, wrote, and hosted a literary salon in Paris

"What is meant by reality? It would seem to be something very erratic, very undependable — now to be found in a dusty road, now in a scrap of newspaper in the street, now a daffodil in the sun."[29]

> Virginia Woolf (1882–1941), English novelist, critic, and essayist

QUANTUM MECHANICS: NOW WHAT'S THE REAL WORLD?

"Those who are not shocked when they first come across quantum theory cannot possibly have understood it."[30]

Niels Bohr (1885–1962), Danish physicist who received the Nobel Prize for Physics in 1922 for his pioneering contributions to modern understandings of atomic structure and quantum mechanics

By the late 19th century, what's now considered old or classical physics had established laws or "facts" of nature which explained quite neatly and seemingly completely how our physical world worked. The "real world" was fixed and known.

But as knowledge advanced and as abilities to observe and measure the physical world improved, bizarre new findings threw the mother of all curve balls at scientists' views of how things really work. Reality shifted yet again.

Quantum mechanics deals with the behavior of matter and energy at the infinitesimally minute level of atoms and subatomic particles. Here's a brief sample of the weird and wonderful discoveries that have emerged since the German physicist Max Planck published his paper in 1900. It ushered in the era of "new physics" or quantum mechanics:

- "Quantum entanglement" shows that two particles can be separated by vast distances and somehow are connected; that manipulation of one particle causes a reaction in the other.
- In the quantum world, particles behave so unpredictably that the best scientists can do is make probability guesses as to what might happen.
- Light behaves like both waves of energy and particles of matter.
- Solid matter doesn't exist. We, and everything around us, are made up of interacting energy or force fields.
- Based on calculations of physical mass in the universe, scientists can only find about 5 percent of the matter needed to hold it all together. A major scientific search is now underway for this "dark matter" and "dark energy," for instance with the 27-kilometer Large Hadron Collider built by the European Organization for Nuclear Research (CERN).
- Some particles travel backward in time. Some appear out of nowhere and then disappear in completely random patterns.
- "Empty spaces" within and between atoms are so full of energy that an area the size of a marble contains more energy than all the solid matter in the known universe.[31]
- Strong evidence suggests that there are seven or more additional dimensions in the universe beyond the known dimensions of width, length, depth (3D), and time.
- Particles can be in two places at once — sometimes even thousands of places at the same time.
- It's impossible to objectively measure quantum behavior. The observer's very presence changes the experiment's outcome.

Talk about the speed of change! We're clearly a long, long way from defining any sort of objective or definite "reality." Reality is a moving target. What's "real" to us today will be considered naïve and laughable to our great-great-ancestors centuries from now.

For All We Know: Creating Our Own Reality

"In the last three decades findings in experimental psychology have suggested that one's belief about the world may actually change it. This idea is very disturbing to the usual conceptions of the mind, suggesting that mind can actually influence events at a distance — that it can 'move matter' and thereby shape the world around us."[32]

Larry Dossey, Recovering the Soul: A Scientific and Spiritual Search (1989)

When we are conscious, we are awake and aware of what's going on around us. Our consciousness creates our thoughts, feelings, and beliefs. When we're unconscious, we may just be asleep or our brain could be injured and shutting down our awareness and feelings (such as pain), as it regulates automatic functions such as our breathing and heartbeat. Alcohol or drugs can alter our consciousness, too, and radically alter our thinking and behaviors.

Most of us can accept that where we focus our own personal consciousness or awareness creates our perception, which then creates our reality. But science is now raising serious questions about whether there is such a thing as objective reality or unchanging facts in this earthly dimension.

Amit Goswami, a physics professor (emeritus) at the University of Oregon and author of ten books, is one of the pioneers in a new multidisciplinary paradigm of science based on the primacy of consciousness. He explains his theory of science within consciousness: "Establishment science is done within the metaphysical umbrella that says that matter is the ground of all being, including mind and consciousness which are brain phenomena. Science within consciousness turns this upside down: consciousness is the ground of all being; matter, including the brain, consists of quantum possibilities of consciousness. When we observe matter, we choose from among these possibilities to produce the actual event that we experience."[33]

What the Bleep Do We Know!?

What the Bleep Do We Know!? is a fascinating film combining documentary-style interviews, computer graphics, and a story of a deaf female photographer, all woven together. It intertwines spiritual questions and themes with concepts of quantum mechanics and consciousness. It challenges many assumptions about how our world — especially the deeper and unseen aspects of it — really works. One reason I highly recommend watching it (go to www.whatthebleep.com for details) is because it will leave you with more questions than answers. Exploring perplexing mysteries should be part of our life's journey.

In their follow-up book, *What the Bleep Do We Know: Discovering the Endless Possibilities for Altering Your Everyday Reality*, the film's three directors and producers cite the research of a number of highly qualified scientists and physicists on the impossibility of objectively measuring what happens at the quantum level of physics. This leads them to conclude, "All of this serves to blur the once-sharp distinction between the 'world out there' and the subjective observer, which seem to merge or dance together in the process of discovering — or is it creating? — the world…
quantum physics has erased the sharp Cartesian distinction between subject and object, observer and observed, that has dominated science for 400 years. In quantum physics, the observer influences the object observed. There are no isolated observers of a mechanical universe, but everything participates in the universe."[34]

PLAYING OUR STRINGS

"String theory is 21st century physics that fell accidentally into the 20th century[35]...Spreading out the particle into a string is a step in the direction of making everything we're familiar with fuzzy. You enter a completely new world where things aren't at all what you're used to... Having those extra dimensions and therefore many ways the string can vibrate in many different directions turns out to be the key to being able to describe all the particles that we see."[36]

Edward Witten (1951–), American theoretical physicist and professor at the Institute for Advanced Study, Princeton, New Jersey; world-leading researcher in superstring theory

String theory is a fast-evolving new branch of theoretical physics combining quantum mechanics and general relativity. The hope is that string theory can provide a "theory of every-thing" that describes all known natural forces such as gravita-tional, electromagnetic, and the various forms of matter in a mathematically complete system. The major problem is that so far, the emerging theories can't be tested.

Here's how Dennis Gaumond describes this new science in his book, *Why is Life?*: "String theory contends that the basic building blocks of the universe are...tiny loops of thread-like filaments, called strings, which are vibrating or oscillating. These loops are truly funda-mental to all matter and forces and are 'uncuttable' or irreducible. Each loop oscillates in a specific way with a specific amount of energy… strings exist at a micro-level so small that it is beyond modern technology. A string is said to be approximately the size of one 'planck length', 10_{33} cm, or one millionth of a billion of a billionth of a billionth of a centimeter. If a single atom were magnified to the size of the entire universe, one planck length would be about the size of an average tree."[37]

String theory is one of the concepts being explored in my hometown of Kitchener-Waterloo (60 miles west of Toronto). The Perimeter Institute for Theoretical Physics was founded in Waterloo in 1999 by Mike Lazaridis, founder and co-CEO of Research in Motion (RIM), maker of the BlackBerry (www.perimeterinstitute.ca). The Perimeter Institute (PI) has over 60 resident researchers and hosts hundreds of international researchers each year for collaborations and workshops. It has even caught the attention of world-renowned theoretical physicist and mathematician Stephen Hawking.

I visited PI, gazed at the walls of blackboards covered with scrawled equations, and tried to understand a sliver of the work these world-class "brainiacs" are doing. That foray and my ongoing reading about the rapidly evolving field of quantum physics confirm what I knew in high school: I am no mathematician!

But the potential impacts of all of the work currently underway to understand and explain reality are endlessly fascinating and incredibly exciting. Physicist Michio Kaku provides a glimpse of how this new theory changes our views of the reality of our world: "When those little strings vibrate, they create notes and we believe those notes are in fact the subatomic particles that we see around us. The melodies that these notes can play out are called 'matter' and when those melodies create symphonies, that's called the 'universe.'"[38]

We are bundles of energy living in a universe vibrating with energy. Our consciousness can alter that energy. By doing so, we alter reality. The implications are mind boggling.

Catching Our Vibes

"I am convinced that there are universal currents of Divine Thought vibrating the ether everywhere and that any who can feel these vibrations is inspired."

Richard Wagner (1813–1883), German composer, conductor, theatre director, and essayist

In 1994, after months of experimenting, Japanese researcher Masaru Emoto developed a technique to take photos of frozen ice crystals. He then began an extensive series of experiments photographing ice crystals from thousands of water samples from a wide variety of sources and conditioning (www. masaru-emoto.net). Some water sample bottles had negative words like hate, kill, or ugly printed on them in a variety of languages. The resulting photos showed crystals that were deformed and ugly. Other bottles had words like joy, beauty, and thank you printed on the sample bottles. The crystals they contained were stunning and often perfectly symmetrical.

In his first book, *New York Times* bestseller *The Hidden Messages in Water*, Emoto recalls, "I particularly remember one photograph. It was the most beautiful and delicate crystal that I had so far seen — formed by being exposed to the words 'love and gratitude.' It was as if the water had rejoiced and celebrated by creating a flower in bloom. It was so beautiful that I can say that it actually changed my life from that moment on."[39]

Emoto founded the Hado institute in Tokyo (www.hado.net). He defines Hado (rhymes with shadow) as "the intrinsic vibrational pattern at the atomic (quantum) level in all matter. The smallest unit of energy. Its basis is the energy of human consciousness."[40]

Emoto's second book, *The True Power of Water: Healing and Discovering Ourselves*, has, like his first, dozens of water crystal photos. The most stunning photos come from positive words written or spoken to the water samples before freezing and photographing. Beautiful crystals are also formed by playing classical or complex music to the samples; the ugly and deformed crystals have been subjected to heavy metal music. (When I called his office in Japan to get permission to show some of these photos in my workshops and presentations, one of Emoto's research assistants emphasized that "Dr. Emoto isn't against heavy metal music.") Water samples that were prayed to — even though the water sample was polluted — also resulted in dazzling crystals.

Emoto's research has led him to conclude that "water faithfully mirrors all the vibrations created in the world, and changes these vibrations into a form that can be seen with the human eye."[41]

Since our human body is about 70 percent water, do we also mirror and manifest the vibrations we surround ourselves with? If so, what kind of reality is that creating in our lives?

LIFE IS AN OPTICAL ILLUSION

"Much of our knowledge of the world is not an elicitation of what 'is,' but rather it is a construction laid atop the world of experience. This is a very difficult concept for many people to grasp. The world that we see and experience seems so palpable and true, and our conceptualizations are so deeply entwined among themselves, that it just seems fantasy to say that the reality I perceive is largely metaphor and construction and is largely projected onto (rather than observed in) the world. These things are generally true, and they are true for many matters of health and medicine."[42]

Daniel Moerman, Meaning, Medicine and the 'Placebo Effect'

A few years ago, I ran into an old acquaintance I hadn't seen for a while. Our short conversation confirmed just why I hadn't — and wouldn't again soon if I could help it. (Thankfully, I have managed that feat.) I started off with, "Hey Phil. How's it going?" His response was, "Oh, you know; same crap, different day." His expletive-laced language was much spicier than that, but you get the picture. He then proceeded to proudly pile up the most recent crap in his life as if inviting me to wallow in it with him.

Our world does have an abundance of crap. There's lots of injustice, inequality, and unfairness. The crap that hits the fan in life is often not evenly distributed. But we get to decide whether to stand in it or not. We decide if we want today to be crappy or happy. If we walk around with our "crap glasses" on, we'll see lots of it. The more crap we look for, the more crap we see. The more crap we see, the more we look for. My friend and fellow perform-ance improvement author/ speaker Peter Jensen, who has a PhD in sports psychology, calls this "opticalrectumitis," which he loosely translates as "having a shitty outlook on life."[43]

Our world also boasts an abundance of beauty, joy, and happiness. Is that where your focus defaults? We choose which glasses to wear each day. We do need to squarely face our issues — the crap — in our lives. Putting on rose-colored glasses and not addressing problems — our moose-on-the-table — means we're deferring and compounding the day of reckoning when we'll do a face plant in the crap.

It's all in how we frame life's problems and possibilities. The vibrational energy we put out to the universe, and the energy frequency we're tuned into, create our reality. There is no objective reality. We don't see the world as it is; we see the world as we are. As the 13th century German theolo-gian, philosopher, and mystic Meister Eckhart put it, "The eye with which I see God, is the eye with which God sees me."

If we continue to think like we've always thought, we'll continue to get what we've always got.

> *If we continue to think like we've always thought, we'll continue to get what we've always got.*

Perception: Do You See What I See?

"The bottom line, at least as far as science has gone up till now, is this: We create the world we perceive. When I open my eyes and look around, it is not 'the world' that I see, but the world my human sensory equipment is able to see, the world my belief system allows me to see, and the world that my emotions care about seeing or not seeing."[44]

What the Bleep Do We Know!?, William Arntz, Betsy Chasse, and Mark Vicente

45

Tilt your head slightly to the left and look at this drawing. Do you see the rabbit? It's facing to the right with its ears tilted horizontally behind its head on the left. Now tilt your head slightly to the right and focus on the duck. It's gazing to the left with its long bill (what just looked like the rabbit's ears) partly open.

Which one is "the real world"? What we see is what we look for.

Perspective: What Frame Are You Using?

"A penny will hide the biggest star in the Universe if you hold it close enough to your eye."

Samuel Grafton (1907–1997), American journalist

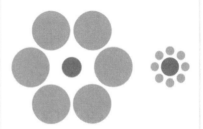

Which dot is larger? It's hard to believe that they are both the same size. But go ahead and measure them. They appear to be different because of how they're framed.

The same thing can be done with a painting. Depending upon the size and color of its frame or matting, the painting can appear larger or smaller, brighter or darker, or imbued with certain colors or tones.

How are you framing turbulence, adversity, or changes in your life? Are you making them bigger or smaller? What color or tone are you accenting? What is the reality that the frames you're using create for you? How do the glasses you've chosen to wear manifest reality in your life?

RANGE OF REALITY: CHOOSING THE BEST OR THE WORST OF TIMES

"It was the best of times, it was the worst of times, it was the age of wisdom, it was the age of foolishness, it was the season of Light, it was the season of Darkness, it was the spring of hope, it was the winter of despair, we had everything before us, we had nothing before us, we were all going direct to Heaven, we were all going direct the other way..."

Charles Dickens (1812–1879), opening lines of A Tale of Two Cities, a historical novel set in London and Paris before and during the French Revolution

With these opening lines, Dickens contrasts the two ends of what I call the Range of Reality. These are the glasses we put on to look at every aspect of our lives all day long. These are the borders we use to look at each situation. These are the focal points for the perspective we bring to our every thought and action hundreds of times throughout any given day.

American Heritage Dictionary provides sharp distinctions for the opposing ends of my Range of Reality:

Pessimism

1. A tendency to stress the negative or unfavorable or to take the gloomiest possible view.
2. The doctrine or belief that this is the worst of all possible worlds and that all things ultimately tend toward evil.
3. The doctrine or belief that the evil in the world outweighs the good.[46]

Optimism

1. A tendency to expect the best possible outcome or dwell on the most hopeful aspects of a situation.
2. The doctrine that this world is the best of all possible worlds.
3. The belief that the universe is improving and that good will ultimately triumph over evil.[47]

RANGE OF REALITY

Pessimism   Optimism

Pessimism		Optimism	
Fearful	Seeing the worst in people	Courageous	Finding the best in people
Negative energy	Unlucky	Positive energy	Lucky
Tuned into bad vibrations	Problem Focused	Tuned into good vibrations	Solution focused
Hopeless	Unhappy	Hopeful	Happy
Impossibility thinking		Possibility thinking	

Martin Seligman is the Robert A. Fox Leadership Professor of Psychology in the University of Pennsylvania's Department of Psychology and director of their Positive Psychology Center. He's been studying optimism and pessimism since his foundational experiments and theories of "learned helplessness" at Cornell University in 1967.

He has written over twenty books on the topic. Here's how he explains and contrasts his more than 40 years of studying pessimism and optimism:

> "Pessimists, I have found… are up to eight times more likely to become depressed when bad events occur; they do worse at school, sports

and most jobs than their talents augur; they have worse physical health and shorter lives; they have rockier inter-personal relations, and they lose American Presidential elections to their more optimistic opponents."[48]

"Optimism and hope are quite well-understood, they have been the objects of thousands of empirical studies, and best of all, they can be built.

Optimism and hope cause better resistance to depression when bad events strike, better performance in work, partic-ularly in challenging jobs, and better physical health."[49]

What's your reality? Where do you choose to spend most of your day on the Range of Reality? These questions are vital for your health, happiness, success, and well-being.

Negative Nuggets: Whining Words of Pessimism

"Life is a sexually transmitted disease."
Anonymous

"She not only expects the worst, but makes the most of it when it happens."
William Hughes Mearns (1875–1965), American educator and poet

"More than any time in history, mankind now faces a crossroads. One path leads to despair and utter hopelessness, the other to total extinction. Let us pray that we have the wisdom to choose correctly."
Woody Allen (1935–), American film director, writer, actor, comedian, musician, and playwright

Pessimist: One who complains about the noise when opportunity knocks.

"If some great catastrophe is not announced every morning, we feel a certain void. 'Nothing in the paper today' we sigh."
Paul Valéry (1871–1945), French poet, essayist, and philosopher

"Life — the way it really is — is a battle not between Bad and Good but between Bad and Worse."
Joseph Brodsky (1940–1996), Russian-born American poet, critic, essayist, dead at 56

"A pessimist's idea of optimism — 'We've hit the lowest point; the situation can't get any worse.' 'No, it can still get worse.'"
Anonymous

Positive Points: Winning Words of Optimism

"Everything works out in the end. If it hasn't worked out, it's not the end."

Our daughter Vanessa's favorite philosophy

"Darkness cannot drive out darkness; only light can do that. Hate cannot drive out hate; only love can do that."

Martin Luther King, Jr. (1929–1968), American clergyman, activist, and prominent leader in the African-American civil rights movement

"Never think of the consequences of failing, you will always think of negative results. Think only positive thoughts and your mind will gravitate towards those thoughts!"

Michael Jordan, retired athlete called by the National Basketball Association "the greatest basketball player of all time"; failed to make his high school varsity basketball team in his sophomore year

"This is the art of courage: to see things as they are and still believe that the victory lies not with those who avoid the bad, but those who taste, in living awareness, every drop of the good."

Victoria Lincoln (1905–1981), "The Art of Courage," Vogue[50]

"Optimism (is)…an inner resource — the ability to believe that times may be rough but that, with renewed effort, they'll improve, that failure and success are to a great degree states of mind."[51]

Steven J. Stein and Howard E. Book, The EQ Edge. Emotional Intelligence and Your Success

"The Green Bay Packers never lost a football game. They just ran out of time."

Vincent Thomas Lombardi (1913–1970), American football coach

The Mind-Body Connection

"The relationship between emotion and health is turning out to be more interesting, and more important, than most of us could have imagined. Viewed through the lens of 21st-century science, anxiety, alienation and hopelessness are not just feelings. Neither are love, serenity and optimism. All are physiological states that affect our health just as clearly as obesity or physical fitness. And the brain, as the source of such states, offers a potential gateway to countless other tissues and organs — from the heart and blood vessels to the gut and the immune system. The challenge is to map the pathways linking mental states to medical ones, and learn how to travel them at will."[52]

> Herbert Benson (Mind/Body Medical Institute Associate Professor of Medicine at Harvard Medical School), Julie Corliss (medical writer at Harvard Medical School), and Geoffrey Cowley (Newsweek's health editor)

"Placebo treatment can dramatically reduce pain compared to no treatment, but only if the subjects know it is happening. It is not the placebo itself that reduces the pain, which makes perfect sense since it is inert. It is the knowledge of the placebo that does the trick... Human biology is comprised of neurons, neurotransmitters and synapses; but it is also comprised of meaning, experience, knowledge and practice."[53]

> Daniel Moerman, Meaning, Medicine and the 'Placebo Effect'

"All the major diseases of our day — heart disease, cancer, hypertension, and more — were shown to be influenced, at least to some degree, by the mind."[54]

> Larry Dossey, Recovering the Soul: A Scientific and Spiritual Search

"My research has shown me that when emotions are expressed — which is to say that the biochemicals that are the substrate of emotion are flowing freely — all systems are united and made whole. When emotions are repressed, denied, not allowed to be whatever they may be, our network pathways get blocked, stopping the flow of the vital feel-good unifying chemicals that run both our biology and our behavior."[55]

> Candace Pert, Molecules of Emotion

"When athletes think they are taking a performance-enhancing drug, their performance tends to get better — even if they never really take the drug. 'This is a very relevant finding of the biology of the mind,' said study co-author Dr. Ken Ho, head of the pituitary research unit at the Garvan Institute of Medical Research in Sydney, Australia. 'There is a very real placebo effect at play in a sporting context, in which a favorable outcome can be achieved purely on the basis of a belief that one has received something beneficial — even if one hasn't.'"[56]

> "Sports Doping's Effect May Be in the Mind," HealthDay

www.JimClemmer.com

- A large selection of articles on Attitude and Outlook at http://www.jimclemmer.com/attitude.
- A selection of my writing and reader discussions on Attitude and Outlook from my **blog** and **monthly newsletter** at http://www.jimclemmer.com/newsletter/?cat=21.

Books

- Chapter Three, "Responsibility for Choices" of *Growing the Distance: Timeless Principles for Personal, Career, and Family Success.*

PART THREE

Real Choices

Slipping down or stepping up.

WALLOW, FOLLOW, OR LEAD

"Be thine own palace, or the world's thy jail."

John Donne (1572–1631), English metaphysical poet

My wife Heather broke her ankle slipping on the ice in our driveway while taking the recycling bins to the curb for pickup. No one heard her cries for help as she lay in excruciating pain. The snow banks prevented any of our neighbors or people driving by from noticing her plight. She resolutely dragged herself back up the frozen driveway to the side door steps. She was yelling for me or our teenage kids, but we couldn't hear her. We were inside the house with the doors and windows sealed tight against the winter deep freeze. She resorted to throwing snowballs and chunks of ice at the door to get someone's attention.

When no one responded, Heather dragged her pain-racked and nearly hypothermic body up the porch stairs and managed to open the door. With more yelling (it's a wonder she could muster the strength), she finally got our attention. Chris and I tried to help her stand up but her pain was too intense. After being rushed to the hospital by ambulance, she had emergency surgery to repair her shattered ankle. She was off work for weeks and took months to fully recuperate.

With her leg in a cast propped up on a chair, she retold her story numerous times to family members and friends during the Christmas holidays. She'd always end by sincerely reflecting on how lucky she was. "I could have easily hit my head on the big rock in the garden beside the driveway and seriously hurt or killed myself," Heather would say. "Or I could have smashed my wrist or broken my arm, too. I was just lucky it happened before everyone went to school or work or the house would have been empty." She often spoke compassionately about how other people in the surgical recovery ward at the hospital were in much worse shape. During her stay, she tried to cheer them up.

Rick broke his leg falling off a ladder when he leaned over too far putting Christmas lights on his house. He lay in agonizing pain among the low shrubs near his front porch. He alternately swore and yelled for help. No one heard him. He threw twigs and snow at the front window but could not get a response. When he tried to move, the extreme pain caused him to faint. He awoke and proceeded to yell and curse himself hoarse. He finally lay back in the snow, growing colder and colder. About two hours later his wife came looking for him. Rick had just enough voice left to scream at her for not getting her butt out there sooner.

At the hospital, Rick complained bitterly about the twenty minutes he had to wait for his diagnosis that surgery would be required. During his recovery, Rick was angry about the food, nurses who didn't respond immediately to his every whim, the other "jerks" in his ward, and the weeks of work he'd miss. He bitterly pronounced that this was "some kind of Christmas present." He reserved his fiercest fury for his wife and kids for not hearing him calling them after his fall. "It figures! You never listen to me."

During his convalescence, friends or family visiting during Christmas holidays repeatedly heard Rick decry the unfairness of his situation. "If it wasn't for bad luck, I'd have no luck at all," he complained. "And, of course, it's my right foot. So I can't even drive the car. But what else would you expect?" He'd provide the litany of activities he was missing out on during the holidays and at work. "And it will take months for me to recover." The only thing that cheered him up was his plan to sue the ladder manufacturer.

Groaning or Growing

"What we see depends on mainly what we look for."
Sir John Lubbock (1834–1913), British banker, politician, and naturalist.

Wallowing	Following	Leading
Pessimism	Cynicism/Skepticism	Optimism
Negative	Neutral	Positive
Fear	Caution	Courage
Hopeless	Helpless	Hopeful
Resists change	Watches change	Leads change
Reactive	Passive	Proactive
Makes excuses	Goes along	Gets results
Impossibility thinking	Probability thinking	Possibility thinking
Complaining about what happened	Watching it happen	Making it happen
Losing perspective	Looking for perspective	Shaping perspective
Whining and complaining	Watching and waiting	Promoting and supporting
Life is mostly sin and evil	Life mostly tolerable	Life is mostly goodness and love
Energy vampire	Energy giver/taker	Energy source

WFL: WHICH FRAMING LEVEL?

"The meaning of things lies not in the things themselves, but in our attitude towards them."

Antoine de Saint Exupery (1900–1944),
French writer and aviator

A central theme in my decades of attempting to understand, apply, synthesize, and teach leadership skills is that leadership is an action, not a position. Leadership is determined by what we do, not the role we play. Whether or not we're truly a leader is determined by what we consistently think and do.

All too many people in leadership roles don't act like leaders. Conversely, many people who haven't been given formal leadership authority are nonetheless very strong leaders. We all need to be leaders — in our personal lives or taking a leading role in our family, communities, profession, relationships, or workplace. Leaders are inspired and inspire others. Leaders take action. Leaders are all about inspir-*action*.

Whether we choose to be leaders or not shines through most clearly when we face turbulence, adversity, or unwanted change. Those trying times often involve suffering or loss. That could be loss of a loved one, our health or physical mobility, a relationship, a job, money, autonomy, control, or status.

During these times we can lead, we can follow, or we can wallow.

We decide which glasses we will put on to view our situation. When we choose how to look at the challenge we're hit with — often unexpectedly — we choose the frame to put around it. That frame makes our situation appear larger or smaller or brighter or darker. These choices create our reality. Bit by bit, these

Leaders take action. Leaders are all about inspir-action.

choices accumulate to create our life. They determine our personal health and happiness as well as our team and organization success.

Everyday Choices

Today I can complain because the weather is rainy or I can be thankful that the grass is getting watered for free.

Today I can feel sad that I don't have more money or I can be glad that my finances encourage me to plan my purchases wisely and guide me away from waste.

Today I can grumble about my health or I can rejoice that I am alive. Today I can lament all that my parents didn't give me when I was growing up or I can feel grateful that thanks to them, I was born.

Today I can cry because roses have thorns or I can celebrate that thorns have roses.

Today I can mourn my lack of friends or I can embark upon an exciting quest to discover new relationships.

Today I can whine because I have to go to work or I can shout for joy because I have a job to do. I can moan because I have to go to school or eagerly open my mind and fill it with rich new tidbits of knowledge.

Today I can gripe because I have to do housework or I can feel thankful because I have shelter.

Today stretches ahead of me, waiting to be shaped. And here I am, the sculptor who gets to do the shaping. What today will be like is up to me. I get to choose what kind of day I will have!

Author Unknown

WFL MODEL: WHICH FRAMING LEVEL?

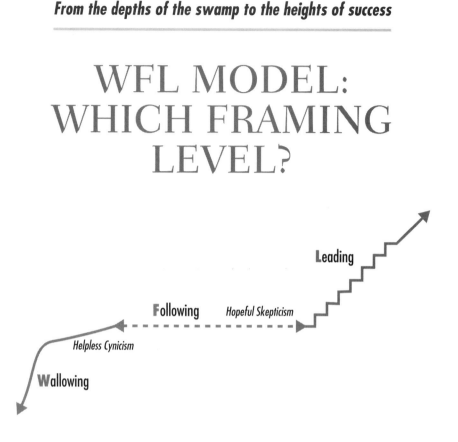

Following

The midpoint — and largest section of this diagram — shows that when faced with a setback, major change, or difficulty, many people sit "on the line" in following mode. Followers may be shocked or stunned. Followers are often waiting to see what else might happen. Followers are looking to others for direction. They may not jump right on the Bitter Bus, but they are at the front of the line to get a good seat. They don't see the glass as half full or half empty but see both sides — or twice as much glass as is required. Typical comments from followers are, "Somebody should do something about this," "I am not sure what to do next," or, "I am just lying low, keeping my head down."

Followers at the right end of the Following spectrum are skeptical but hopeful. They could be wisely analyzing the situation to understand what happened and what their options might be in dealing with it. To avoid being on the "bleeding edge" of change or jumping in too quickly with a ready-fire-aim approach, they could be weighing how to respond. With the right encouragement or positive influence, they're close to stepping up to deal with the situation.

At the left or cynical end of the Following scale, followers are feeling helpless and cynical. With a slight push or just a bit more negative influence, they'll start to slide down the slippery slope of cynical pessimism.

Wallowing

The greasy downgrade of negativity and cynicism can very quickly skid over a cliff into the swamp of despair and helplessness. Wallowers take a bad situation and make it worse.

Wallowers "blamestorm" rather than brainstorm in their search for someone to point the finger at. Wallowers crave certainty and long for the "good old days" — which they used to complain about incessantly and would resent actually returning to. Wallowers hate "now" and want to be anywhere other than in the present moment. Wallowers are overwhelmed by the problem and narrow their field of vision to few or no options.

Wallowers live in a world of hurt and worry. In positions of power, they use fear to "motivate" and manipulate. Wallowers believe most people are incompetent and can't be trusted; they focus on weaknesses and gaps. Wallowers use punishment, criticism, and threats to shove others toward higher performance. Bullies are usually wallowers. Wallowers set up destructive magnetic energy fields of negative vibrations.

Wallowers often play the victim. Their world is full of conspiracies with lots of "they" talk; "They are out to get us";

> *Wallowers use punishment, criticism, and threats to shove others toward higher performance.*

"They don't understand"; "They never listen to us." Wallowers routinely ride the Bitter Bus down Helpless Highway through Frown Town past Pessimism Place, Whining Way, and Dead End Drive into Pity City. Many wallowers drive the Bitter Bus and actively recruit fence-sitting followers to join them.

Leading

Taking the leadership stairs is the way to rise above and master the situation. Leaders take the initiative to make the best of the bad hand that's been dealt. Leaders often live with ambiguity and paradox while exploring and creating a broad array of options. Leaders try to live in the moment while building for the future. Leaders believe most people are competent and trustworthy until proven otherwise. Leaders assume good intent. Leaders look for the best in people and focus on reinforcing and leveraging everyone's strengths.

Leaders face tough times squarely. They don't sugarcoat things or flee from difficult situations or touchy conversations. Leaders bring hope by focusing beyond what is to what could be. Leaders are self-aware and build disciplined habits of continuous improvement. Leaders are grateful and look for opportunities to celebrate and recognize progress. Leaders praise and encourage others on to higher performance. Leaders set up affirmative magnetic energy fields of positive vibrations. Leaders are "inspir-*actional*."

Leaders are navigators and say, "I am going to do something about this"; "How can we capitalize on this change?"; "We've overcome problems before and we can do it again." Leaders drive the Success Express and recruit followers to hop on board the Better Bus as they cruise on Positive Parkway through Joyful Junction and Happy Hamlet past Peak Performance Place, past Winner's Circle, and into Pretty City.

Okay; I can tell you've had enough Dad Jokes in this section!

> *Leaders believe most people are competent and trustworthy until proven otherwise.*

Winning Words: Perspectives on Choosing our Perspective

"In the final analysis it becomes clear that the sort of person the prisoner became was the result of an inner decision and not the result of camp influences alone. Fundamentally, therefore, any man can, even under such circumstances, decide what shall become of him — mentally and spiritually. He may retain his human dignity even in a concentration camp."[57]

Viktor Emil Frankl (1905–1997), Austrian neurologist, psychiatrist, and Holocaust survivor, Man's Search for Meaning

"Consider these statements: 'I have not done it' or, 'I don't think they should do it' or, 'I don't believe I could do it' or, 'I don't want to do it.' Each of these statements contains an element of personal responsibility that does not use what others have done as an excuse. Contrast those statements with: 'They shouldn't even try to participate in decisions' or, 'Nobody around here could ever do that' or, 'They would never let us get involved.' These statements assign responsibility for actions to some higher authority…"[58]

Geoffrey M. Bellman, Getting Things Done When You Are Not in Charge

"People with an external locus of control see the world as controlling them; they are subject to the forces of other people, chance, or of 'fate.' Obviously, both conditions exist at the same time; I determine if I will brush my teeth this morning or not, but I also recognize that there is precious little I can do about the Chinese government's one-child policy or the weather. But the proportion of things which individuals put in each category can vary quite dramatically, and this factor has been shown to be related to a number of different aspects of health and stress."[59]

Daniel Moerman, Meaning, Medicine and the 'Placebo Effect'

"God grant me the senility to forget the people I never liked anyway, the good fortune to run into the ones I do, and the eyesight to tell the difference. Amen."

Author Unknown

PAYOFFS OF TAKING THE LEAD

"In the long run, we shape our lives,
and we shape ourselves. The process never ends
until we die. And the choices we make are
ultimately our own responsibility."

(Anna) Eleanor Roosevelt (1884–1962),
American diplomat, writer, U.S. First Lady

It's been said that we can't direct the wind, but we can adjust our sails. The wallower curses the wind, the follower waits for it to change, and the leader adjusts the sails. A rapidly multiplying body of research proves that the payoffs of choosing to adjust ourselves and lead above the line are massive. Here's just the tip of a very deep iceberg:

- "An upbeat environment fosters mental efficiency, making people better at taking in and understanding information, at using decision rules in complex judgements, and at being flexible in their thinking."[60]

- "Teaching ten-year-old children the skills of optimistic thinking and action cuts their rate of depression in half when they go through puberty."[61]

- "A study of insurance salespeople (shows) a 56 percent sales advantage among the optimists."[62]

- "Optimistic managers are more likely to be engaged managers who are more likely to engage employees; engaged employees, in turn, are more optimistic and productive than disengaged employees, and their increased productivity increases profitability."[63]

- "Of the fifty-four couples, sixteen divorced or separated over the four years, and the more positive their explanations (Ed. note: explanations about/for their partner, i.e., "he was tired" vs. "he was in a bad mood"), the more likely they were to stay together. The upshot of this is straightforward. Optimism helps marriage."[64]

- Optimists report a higher level of physical and mental functioning than pessimists, according to Mayo Clinic researchers. "The wellness of being is not just physical but attitudinal," says Dr. Toshihiko Maruta.[65]

> *...the pay-offs of choosing to adjust ourselves and lead above the line are massive.*

- "...optimists had 19 percent greater longevity, in terms of their expected life span, compared to that of the pessimists."[66]

- "Men with high levels of optimism had less than half the risk for combined fatal and nonfatal myocardial infarction and for angina pectoris. The greater their optimism, the lower the risk for cardiac incidents."[67]

- "Managers who got sick or who sank to low performance displayed a sense of alienation: they felt externally controlled, often overwhelmed or helpless, and tried to find security by regressing and turning situations back to the way they were."[68]

Optimism is the ultimate anti-depressant.

COGNITIVE PSYCHOLOGY: CHOOSING OUR REALITY

*"**Cognition:** The process of knowing and, more precisely, the process of being aware, knowing, thinking, learning, and judging."*

MedicineNet.com

Back in the mideighties when I was leading The Achieve Group (now part of AchieveGlobal), Peter Strickland introduced me to the work of Martin Seligman. I was working on my first book, *The VIP Strategy: Leadership Skills for Exceptional Performance* with Achieve cofounder, Art McNeil. We had just hired Peter to head up the trainer-training part of our business associated with Zenger Miller's programs (also now part of AchieveGlobal). Peter knew I was looking for credible research on the links between self-determination, optimism,

and leadership.

I became an avid follower of Seligman's leading-edge work at the University of Pennsylvania. He began his distinguished psychology career in the late sixties studying pessimism, learned helplessness, and depression. In 1990 Seligman released his seminal book, *Learned Optimism*.[69] It is loaded with extensive and solid research from the rapidly expanding field of cognitive therapy — within the larger field of cognitive behavioral therapies. *Learned Optimism* proved that "optimism is essential for a good and successful life." This very practical book is an excellent introduction to the power of cognitive therapy and provides very useful self-assessment tools followed by plenty of suggestions for building optimism at work, as parents with our kids, in schools, in sports, in organizations, and for our own health.

For most of the nineties, *Learned Optimism* was my favorite book on personal growth and self-leadership. Here are a few of its key points that are relevant to how we choose the frames that create our reality:

- Pessimistic prophecies are self-fulfilling and create a downward spiral — often into depression.
- Depression is a symptom of conscious negative thinking and does not come from underlying disorders, unresolved issues, unconscious anger, or brain chemistry.
- Pessimism is not fixed and unchangeable. Anyone can become optimistic by learning a new set of cognitive skills.
- Our thoughts aren't just reactions to events; they often change what causes or follows those events.
- Self-direction rather than outside forces explains our actions and gives us control over our lives.
- For the first time in history, a large number of people have a significant amount of choice — societal rights, in fact — and personal control over their lives.
- During a time of dramatic increases in material wealth, severe depression is ten times worse in North America than 50 years ago.
- We all have automatic thoughts or styles of explanation that we try to impose on others for the good and bad events in our lives.
- Our explanatory style develops in childhood and determines whether we're pessimistic or optimistic (wallowing, following, or leading ourselves and others).
- Cognitive behavioral therapy can permanently reset our explanatory style to optimism, with a low relapse rate.
- Attitude, motivation, and optimism are key predictors of future success.
- Sports teams with optimistic explanatory styles perform better.
- Optimistic U.S. presidential candidates win more elections.

Buddha Was a Cognitive Psychologist

"All that we are is the result of what we have thought. The mind is everything. What we think, we become."

Gautama Buddha (c. 563–483 BC), "Awakened One" or "Enlightened One"

There are countless pathways to understanding and changing our thinking patterns. I've long been studying and applying some of the teachings of Buddhism as part of my spiritual journey and reframing life's challenges. Morning spiritual reading and prayer/meditation have been key parts of my day for decades. Two of the many books I've found useful in my practice have been German-Canadian writer Eckhart Tolle's *The Power of Now* and *A New Earth*. His books are not explicitly about Buddhism, but modernize and make accessible some of the principles of this spiritual path.

In 2005, Aaron Beck, a psychiatrist and the founder of cognitive therapy in the early 1960s, met the Dalai Lama to compare the core principles of cognitive therapy with Buddhism. Beck also gave the Dalai Lama a copy of his book, *Prisoners of Hate*, which outlined his findings that hatred imprisons individuals who harbor it.

The two agreed on these fascinating overlaps between their two approaches:

Similarities between Cognitive Therapy and Buddhism

I. Goals: Serenity, Peace of Mind, Relief of Suffering

II. Values:

(1) Importance of Acceptance, Compassion, Knowledge, Understanding

(2) Altruism vs. Egoism

(3) Universalism vs. Groupism: "We are one with all humankind."

(4) Science vs. Superstition

(5) Self-responsibility

III. Causes of Distress:

(1) Egocentric biases leading to excessive or inappropriate anger, envy, cravings, etc. (the "toxins") and false beliefs ("delusions")

(2) Underlying self-defeating beliefs that reinforce biases

(3) Attaching negative meanings to events

IV. Methods:

(1) Focus on the Immediate (here and now)

(2) Target the biased thinking through
(a) Introspection
(b) Reflectiveness
(c) Perspective-taking
(d) Identification of "toxic" beliefs
(e) Distancing
(f) Constructive experiences
(g) Nurturing "positive beliefs"

(3) Use of Imagery

(4) Separating distress from pain

(5) Mindfulness training[70]

EXPLANATORY STYLE: DON'T P AND SHOULD YOURSELF

"Pessimists have a particularly pernicious way of construing their setbacks and frustrations. They automatically think that the cause is permanent, pervasive and personal: 'It's going to last forever, it's going to undermine everything, and it's my fault.'... Optimists, in contrast, have a strength that allows them to interpret their setbacks as surmountable, particular to a single problem, and resulting from temporary circumstances or other people."[71]

Martin Seligman, Authentic Happiness: Using the
New Positive Psychology to Realize Your
Potential for Lasting Fulfillment

It's all too easy to listen to others tell us how we "should" feel about positive or negative events in our lives. We think and act according to our deep-rooted habits about what we think we "should" do in response. Unless we become more aware of our own thoughts, we don't realize how automatic — and possibly destructive — they've become.

The "three Ps" of permanence, pervasiveness, and personalization define our explanatory style. Our explanatory style establishes the glasses or frames through which we create reality. If we build the skills or habits of using a positive or leading style, the three Ps are a stairway to ever higher effectiveness in our personal and professional lives. If we've habitually chosen a negative or wallowing style, we slide ever deeper into the swamp of unhappiness and despair.

The good news is that you can stop P-ing and should'ing yourself! But after years of walking around with "optical-rectumitis" — and maybe even wet pants — it's not easy to change your crap glasses. You may need a coach, mentor, training, therapy, a support group, structured personal growth program, or other such help. This book is designed to give you the inspiration and action ideas to guide you toward a positive change of your reality optics.

PERMANENCE

EXPLAINING BAD EVENTS:

Permanent (Pessimistic/Wallowing)

"I am a loser."
"My boss is a jerk."
"You're always late."

Temporary (Optimistic/Leading)

"I was really off my game today."
"My boss really messed up this time."
"You've been late three times in the past week."

EXPLAINING GOOD EVENTS:

Temporary (Pessimistic/Wallowing)

"I caught a lucky break."
"Looks like they gave in on this one."
"My competitor messed up."

Permanent (Optimistic/Leading)

"My luck's holding up again."
"I am persistent."
"My service is clearly better."

PERVASIVENESS

EXPLAINING BAD EVENTS:

Universal (Pessimistic/Wallowing)

"All (managers/workers/_____) are idiots."
"I am a terrible parent."
"All instructions and help programs are useless."

Specific (Optimistic/Leading)

"He was really off the mark on this one."
"Our teenager is going through a tough phase."
"These instructions are very poorly written."

EXPLAINING GOOD EVENTS:

Specific (Pessimistic/Wallowing)	Universal (Optimistic/Leading)
"I am good at problem-solving."	*"I am a strong leader."*
"Our team really pulled together."	*"We're an effective team."*
"I was persuasive."	*"I am a good communicator."*

PERSONALIZATION

EXPLAINING BAD EVENTS:

Hopeless (Wallowing)	Hopeful (Leading)
"I am just not smart enough."	*"Emotional Quotient (EQ) is much more important than Intellectual Quotient (IQ)."*
"Just like a man/woman."	*"I caught him/her at a bad time."*
"With my luck, this is likely cancer."	*"The odds are in my favor and this is likely benign."*

EXPLAINING GOOD EVENTS:

Hopeless (Wallowing)	Hopeful (Leading)
"We barely made it this time."	*"We're good."*
"I wonder what my spouse is really up to."	*"My spouse is considerate."*
"That was a lucky fluke."	*"I am lucky."*

You can override your nature and nurture:
Happiness is an inside job.

POSITIVE PSYCHOLOGY AND HAPPINESS

"Happiness does not depend on outward conditions.
It depends on inner conditions. It isn't what
you have, who you are, where you are, or what you
are doing that makes you happy or unhappy.
It is what you think about it."

Dale Carnegie (1888–1955), How to Win Friends
and Influence People, *American writer, speaker, and*
developer of self-improvement courses

In 1996, Martin Seligman was elected president of the American Psychological Association by a landslide. This set him casting about for a central theme for his time in this key leadership role. A few weeks later — still puzzling over a theme — he was weeding in his garden. His five-year-old daughter, Nikki, was throwing weeds in the air and singing. This distraction caused Seligman to yell at her to stop. A few minutes later she came and said, "Daddy, I want to talk to you."

"Yes, Nikki?"

"Daddy, do you remember before my fifth birthday? From when I was three until I was five, I was a whiner. I whined every day. On my fifth birthday, I decided I wasn't going to whine anymore. That was the hardest thing I have ever done.

And if I can stop whining, you can stop being such a grouch."

From the mouths of babes!

Seligman describes this encounter in his outstanding book, *Authentic Happiness: Using the New Positive Psychology to Realize Your Potential for Lasting Fulfillment*. His encounter with Nikki is described in an early chapter entitled "How Psychology Lost its Way and I Found Mine." Seligman writes of his conversation with Nikki, "This was an epiphany for me….I'd spent fifty years enduring mostly wet weather in my soul and the last ten years as a walking nimbus cloud in a household radiant with sunshine …in that moment I resolved to change…raising children, I know now…was far more than just fixing what was wrong with them. It was about identifying and amplifying their strengths and virtues, and helping them find the niche where they can live those positive traits to the fullest."[72]

Seligman, who elsewhere in that book described himself as a natural pessimist studying optimism, has authored 20 books and 170 articles on motivation and personality. This turning point with Nikki led him to found the Positive Psychology movement. Here's an excerpt from the Positive Psychology Center spawned by Seligman's pioneering leadership of this rapidly growing movement:

> "*Positive Psychology has three central concerns: positive emotions, positive individual traits, and positive institutions. Understanding positive emotions entails the study of contentment with the past, happiness in the present, and hope for the future. Understanding positive individual traits consists of the study of the strengths and virtues, such as the capacity for love and work, courage, compassion, resilience, creativity, curiosity, integrity, self-knowledge, moderation, self-control, and wisdom. Understanding positive institutions entails the study of the strengths that foster better communities, such as justice, responsibility, civility, parenting, nurturance, work ethic, leadership, teamwork, purpose, and tolerance.*"[73]

This new approach has been at the forefront of explosive levels of research on happiness and leveraging strengths. In *Authentic Happiness*, Seligman provides this useful formula to help us determine "what you can change and what you can't" (the title of one of his earlier books):

$$H = S + C + V$$

Our enduring level of **H**appiness is a result of our **S**et Range plus our **C**ircumstances and **V**oluntary Control. We can't do much about our **S**et Range. It's how we showed up on this earth. **C**ircumstance is a grayer area. Some circumstances — such as our childhood, country of birth, ethnicity, and key people in our lives — we

Just My Luck

"Luck is another name for tenacity of purpose."

Ralph Waldo Emerson (1803–1882), American essayist, philosopher, poet, and leader of the early 19th century transcendentalist movement

Luckily, I caught Richard Wiseman in a radio interview late one night on my way home from the airport. When I got home, I immediately looked him up on the Internet and ordered his book. Wiseman is Professor of the Public Understanding of Psychology at the University of Hertfordshire in the United Kingdom. He's been extensively studying luck over a number of years by interviewing and running experiments with very lucky people who seem to lead charmed lives and very unlucky people who seem to have their own black cloud following them around.

His findings are further proof that we make choices to wallow in and create our own bad luck, or lead ourselves toward attracting "lucky" breaks in our lives.

In his book *The Luck Factor: Change Your Luck and Change Your Life*, Wiseman outlines four principles he has found define lucky people. Through his "luck school," he's retrained up to 80 percent of the unlucky to reverse their fortunes and attract good luck. His four principles involve key elements of leading: engage others in conversations and social interaction; listen to your intuition and trust hunches; develop positive expectations inherited. Our Circumstances factor gets fuzzier when we look at how today's situation is also in large part based on past decisions we've made. The most hopeful aspect of this whole formula — and the core of framing our life in leader mode — is Voluntary Control. Regardless of what's come before or where we are now, we can change our present reality by what we focus upon. And that will bring us a different future.

Seligman's web site, www.authentichappiness.com, has a series of free assessment tools and plenty of practical ideas to help you climb the leadership stairway.

about the future; and strengthen resilience and persistence to eventually turn bad luck into good.

These few excerpts of his luck research further illustrate the magnetic power of the energy force fields we choose in framing, explaining, and acting on the good and bad events in our lives:

- "My research revealed that the special kind of expectations held by lucky and unlucky people had a huge impact on their lives. The unique way that lucky people thought about their future was responsible for them being more effective than most when it came to achieving their dreams and ambitions. Likewise, the unlucky expectations held by unlucky people resulted in them being especially ineffectual at getting what they wanted from life."[74]

- "Lucky people see any bad luck in their lives as being very short lived. They simply shrug it off and don't let it affect their expectations about the future. Unlucky people are convinced that any good luck in their lives will only last for a short period of time, and will quickly be followed by their regular dose of bad luck."[75]

- "Luck was not a magical ability or a gift from the gods. Instead, it was a state of mind: a way of thinking and behaving. People are not born lucky or unlucky, but create much of their own good and bad luck through their thoughts, feelings and actions."[76]

In a hurricane, it's the palm tree that survives.

HARDINESS AND RESILIENCE: WHEN GIVING IN CAN GIVE US A LIFT

"Our greatest glory is not in never falling, but in rising every time we fall."

Confucius (551–479 BC), Chinese thinker and social philosopher

We tend to think of unwavering steadfastness and never-say-die persistence as important leadership qualities. To a point they are. But resilience in the face of the hurricane-force winds of change is as often about being flexible like a palm tree rather than unbending like an oak.

Like so much of life, it's about balance. W.C. Fields was on to something about resilience when he quipped, "If at first you don't succeed, try again. Then quit. No use being a damn fool about it." Sometimes the wisest thing to do is to let it storm, find shelter, and look for an alternate route to our dream. Maybe it wasn't even the right dream; we may need to accept what the universe is trying to tell us and reset our destination.

Psychologists Gregory Miller and Carsten Wrosch contrasted and studied people who are relentless and unbending and people who accept and flex with life's twists and turns. They found that flexible people were much healthier than their steadfast counterparts. Stress levels were quite a bit lower, and a protein indicating bodily inflammation linked to diabetes and heart disease was much lower. The flexible, resilient group was able to bounce back more effectively from serious defeats, less likely to dwell on the past, set new goals, and get on with their lives.[77]

Leading Research and Hardy Perspectives

"The leaders I met, whatever walk of life they were from, whatever institutions they were presiding over, always referred back to the same failure, something that happened to them that was personally difficult, even traumatic, something that made them feel that desperate sense of hitting bottom — as something they thought was almost a necessity. It's as if at that moment the iron entered their soul; that moment created the resilience that leaders need."[78]

Warren Bennis, Distinguished Professor of Business Administration and Founding Chairman of The Leadership Institute at the University of Southern California

"I never blame myself when I'm not hitting. I just blame the bat and if it keeps up, I change bats. After all, if I know it isn't my fault that I'm not hitting, how can I get mad at myself?"

Yogi Berra (1925–), former Major League Baseball player and manager

"Resilient people and companies face reality with staunchness, make meaning of hardship instead of crying out in despair, and improvise solutions from thin air. Others do not...We all know people who, under duress, throw up their hands and cry, 'How can this be happening to me?' Such people see themselves as victims, and living through hardship carries no lessons for them. But resilient people devise constructs about their suffering to create some sort of meaning for themselves and others...an increasing body of empirical evidence shows that resilience — whether in children, survivors of concentration camps, or businesses back from the brink — can be learned."[79]

Diane L. Coutu, "How Resilience Works," Harvard Business Review

"Really negative events have the ability to shake up the status quo in your life, which opens the door for change. You could become a depressed, despairing drunk — or you could become a much better person."[80]

W. Keith Campbell, professor of social psychology at the University of Georgia

"More than education, more than experience, more than training, a person's level of resilience will determine who succeeds and who fails. That's true in the cancer ward, it's true in the Olympics, and it's true in the boardroom."

Dean Becker, president and CEO of Adaptiv Learning Systems[81]

www.JimClemmer.com

- A large selection of articles on Attitude and Outlook at http://www.jimclemmer.com/attitude.
- A selection of my writing and reader discussions on Attitude and Outlook from my **blog** and **monthly newsletter** at http://www.jimclemmer.com/newsletter/?cat=21.

Books

- Chapter Three, "Responsibility for Choices" of *Growing the Distance: Timeless Principles for Personal, Career, and Family Success.*
- Self-assessment, application ideas, and personal planning exercises in the "Responsibility for Choices" section of *Growing the Distance: Self-Study System.*
- For supervisors, managers, and executives – Chapter Three, "Responsibility for Choices" of *The Leader's Digest: Timeless Principles for Team and Organization Success.*
- Management team assessments, application ideas, and planning exercises in the "Responsibility for Choices" section of *The Leader's Digest: Practical Application Planner.*

IV

It's a bitter swill to wallow.

BOGGED DOWN: WHEN WE WALLOW IN THE SWAMP

To wallow

1. *To roll one's self about, as in mire; to tumble and roll about; to move lazily or heavily in any medium; to flounder; as, swine wallow in the mire.*
   'With Smithers out of the picture I was free to wallow in my own crapulence.'

2. *To roll; especially, to roll in anything defiling or unclean.*

3. *To live in filth or gross vice; to disport one's self in a beastly and unworthy manner.*

Wiktionary.org

Life's most turbulent times or traumatic losses are major choice points. Do we ultimately become better or bitter? Do we climb the leadership stairs to a higher state of awareness and appreciation or do we slide down into the quagmire of hopelessness and despair?

The International Committee for the Study of Victimization looked at large groups of people who had experienced major traumatic events. These included prisoners of war, accident victims, cancer patients, survivors of large-scale natural disasters, and the like. Years after the ordeals, they found that the survivors fell into three broad categories: "those who were permanently dispirited by the event, those who got their life back to normal, and those who used the experience as a defining event that made them stronger."[82]

Our response to the Richter-scale shocks that life throws at us can cause seismic reality shifts. When the quake hits — often when we least expect it — most of us experience one, two, or all three of the first steps of the SARAA formula. Whether we successfully get to step five depends upon whether we choose to wallow, follow, or lead.

5. **A**ction
---------------- *(Major choice point)*
4. **A**cceptance
3. **R**esentment
2. **A**nger
1. **S**hock

The first three steps are below the line, in the wallowing swamp. They are also part of the grieving process that we may need to experience in order to let go of what was, face what is (step four), and move ourselves onward and upward with our lives (step five). If we eventually manage to climb the leadership stairway after the major setback or loss, we'll often reflect back on the experience. "It was the best thing that ever happened to me." "It made me stronger." "I appreciate life more now." "It reset my priorities to what's really important." "I don't sweat the small stuff any more." "It forced us to make the changes we really needed to make." "It shocked us out of our complacency."

Steps one through three can be a time of emotional readjustment or healthy venting. But to get bogged down in any one of these stages is to stew in the swamp and begin breathing in the toxic vapors. We may find ourselves on an occasional detour through the emotional quagmire of why-me and this-isn't-fair, but to languish there is deadly to our health, happiness, and success.

Learned Helplessness: The Pike Syndrome

"A much more pernicious loss of choice and control is brought about by repeated failure. After a number of experiences in which our efforts are futile, many of us will give up….learned helplessness then generalizes to situations where the person can, in fact, exercise control. Even when solutions are available, a mindless sense of futility prevents a person from reconsidering the situation."[83]

Ellen J. Langer (1947–), Harvard University psychologist

Since the midsixties, there have been a large number of experiments with animals and people revealing that helplessness can be a conditioned or learned response. An early experiment with learned help-lessness was demonstrated with rats. When they were put directly in ice water, they could swim around for 40 to 60 hours. But if the rats were held until they stopped struggling and then placed into the ice water, they gave up immediately and drowned.

In another case, scientists put a pike in a large aquarium with smaller fish that it feeds upon. However, the pike was separated from its tasty meals by a layer of glass. At first, the pike continuously smashed its head against the glass to reach its prey. Eventually it abandoned the painful and futile attempts. It sank to the bottom of the tank and just lay there. At that point, the scientists removed the glass partition. But the pike now ignored the smaller fish, even when they swam right next to it. Eventually, the pike starved to death, despite its meals being right in front of its pointy nose. This behavior came to be known as "The Pike Syndrome."[84]

Many wallowing people, teams, and sometimes entire organizations choose to become victims of The Pike Syndrome. Here are common examples:

PERSONAL HELPLESSNESS	COLLECTIVE HELPLESSNESS
• That's just the way I am…	• Forget it! We tried that before…
• There's nothing I can do…	• The collective agreement won't let us…
• He/she makes me so mad…	• Management/staff/head office/ customers/operations/sales … don't listen to us…
• They won't allow it…	
• Nobody ever listens to me…	• The systems/policies won't let us….
• I am no good at….	• It's deeply ingrained in our culture…

Statements like these are sometimes a legitimate, healthy acceptance of barriers or limitations blocking the way. We may be better off to just drop it and move on to something else. But in most cases, statements like these are just excuses to give up. Generally, these permanent, pervasive, and personal explanations are

conditioned responses from past failures or setbacks. Like the pike, we may have smashed our noses against the glass ceiling or wall a few times and stopped trying. When conditions change and those barriers are removed or reduced, pessimistic people and teams still wallow helplessly and give up.

One Bad Apple Can Rot the Team

Terence Mitchell, professor of management, organization, and psychology at the University of Washington Business School, along with doctoral student William Felps "analyzed about two dozen published studies that focused on how teams and groups of employees interact, and specifically how having bad teammates can destroy a good team." They concluded:

- "A single 'toxic' or negative team member can be the catalyst for downward spirals in organizations."
- "…in one study of about 50 manufacturing teams…teams that had a member who was

disagreeable or irresponsible were much more likely to have conflict, have poor communication within the team and refuse to cooperate with one another. Consequently, the teams performed poorly."

- "…negative behavior outweighs positive behavior — that is, a 'bad apple' can spoil the barrel but one or two good workers can't unspoil it."
- "Companies need to move quickly to deal with such problems because the negativity of just one individual is pervasive and destructive and can spread quickly."[85]

Pessimism: Make it grow away.

DEADLY DISEASES: VICTIMITIS VIRUS AND PESSIMISM PLAGUE

"Attitudes are contagious. Mine might kill you."

Despair.com

One of the best cruises Heather and I have taken was through the Panama Canal. I hadn't known a lot about this engineering marvel before this trip. Between onboard lectures by a retired geography professor, narration through the canal from a Panama tour guide during the day, and reading David McCullough's highly entertaining and thoroughly researched book, *The Path Between the Seas: The Creation of the Panama Canal 1870–1914*, I learned a lot more about this fascinating story.

The Panama Canal is a tale of scandal, intrigue, blundering, and politics. It's also a tale of visionary leadership, methodical problem-solving, daring innovation, and dogged persistence. Many key people climbed the leadership stairs to break through barriers to what was thought possible. A key piece in the puzzle was solving the deadly scourges of yellow fever and malaria that killed tens of thousands of workers and were huge obstacles to progress. Until a U.S. army doctor, Colonel William Crawford Gorgas, brought his scientific methods to the problem, a prominent belief was that the diseases emanated from mysterious swamp gases. Building on other studies of yellow fever and malaria control efforts in the late 19th century, Gorgas showed that controlling mosquitoes carrying the malaria virus was the key to combating the diseases.

A cornerstone of modern medicine and the dramatically improved health we enjoy in most of the world today is "germ theory," or "the pathogenic theory of medicine." This approach's success is built upon the understanding that microorganisms are the cause of many diseases and can be controlled by antibiotics and hygiene practices. But this is a fairly recent understanding. During much of the 19th century, it was controversial and considered nonsense by many medical experts. In their ignorance, doctors of the time would go directly from autopsies into surgeries or childbirths, unknowingly spreading disease and death.

A burgeoning mountain of studies shows that pessimism dramatically increases sickness and depression, and hastens death. Future historians will likely look back to our day and marvel at our unhygienic practices of "emotional germ theory." Here are a few examples of how the Victimitis Virus and Pessimism Plague are verbally spread around:

- *"Ninety percent of everything is crap."*
- *"Avoid wearing clean underwear; it will only tempt car accidents."*
- *"Stoop and you'll be stepped on; stand tall and you'll be shot at."*
- *"I no longer need to punish, deceive, or compromise myself, unless I want to stay employed."*
- *"If you can remain calm, you don't have all the facts."*
- *"Expect nothing and never be disappointed."*
- *"Some people are alive because it's illegal to kill them."*
- *"If you haven't got something good to say about anyone, come and sit by me."*
  Alice Roosevelt Longworth (1884–1980), oldest child of U.S president Theodore Roosevelt
- *"Maybe this world is another planet's hell."*
  Aldous Leonard Huxley (1894–1963), English writer

- *"I'm tired of this back-slapping, 'aren't humanity neat' bullshit. We're a virus with shoes, okay? That's all we are…. I don't mean to sound bitter, cold, or cruel, but I am, so that's how it comes out."*
  Bill Hicks (1961–1994), American comedian who died at 33

Know Your Energy Vampires

Psychiatrist and Assistant Clinical Professor of psychiatry at University of California Los Angeles (UCLA), Judith Orloff, is a pioneer in the nascent field of energy psychiatry. She is the author of *Positive Energy:10 Extraordinary Prescriptions for Transforming Fatigue, Stress and Fear Into Vibrancy, Strength and Love.* She identifies six types of energy vampires:

Sob Sister (or Brother) — exhausts you with a litany of complaints and problems. She doesn't really want solutions; she just wants to suck out your energy.

Blamer — makes you feel guilty through berating and sometimes verbal abuse.

Drama Queen — exaggerates small problems into big ones. Life is either incredibly good or unbearably bad.

Constant Talker or Joke Teller — has no interest in your feelings. Demands center stage with his exhausting stream of stories, opinions, and jokes.

Fixer-Upper — tries to make you a personal therapist to solve his or her problems.

Go-for-the-Jugular Fiend — a malicious and very negative vampire looking to hurt and cut you down. Driven by envy, competition, and severe insecurity.[86]

Don't let the winds of change fan the flames of fear.

THE FEAR FACTOR: DARK ENERGY FROM THE DARK SIDE

"The only thing we have to fear is fear itself."
Franklin D. Roosevelt (1882–1945), U.S. president in his first inaugural address, 1933, as the country faced the Depression

It's hard to truly comprehend what a powerfully negative force fear is in our lives. Fear emanates from the dark side. Fear is at the root of hatred and evil. Fear is the source of stress and worry. Fear keeps us from speaking up. Fear causes us to pull back and give up. Fear reduces our field of awareness. Fear floods our thoughts with bleak fantasies of failure and destruction. Fear sets up dark energy fields attracting to us that which we most fear. Fear feeds mistrust and destroys relationships. Fear drives abuse and cruelty. Fear erects walls and closes ears. Fear craves power and demands compliance. Fear fosters bullying and abuse of position power. Fear is afraid of participation, transparency, and openness. Fear does not own up to mistakes. Fear shuts down learning. Fear creates the zero-sum thinking that leads to a scarcity mentality. A scarcity mentality leads to greed and hoarding. Fear breeds conflict. Wallowers live in fear.

My sixth book, *Moose on the Table®: A Novel Approach to Communications @ Work*, centered on a fictional character, Pete Leonard, as he allowed fear to seep deep into his life and slowly choke his effectiveness and happiness. Eventually, he found the steps leading out of the slippery pits of fear to soar high above the "getting-by line" to the heights of success.

While writing that book, I engaged in a series of stimulating discussions with readers of my monthly newsletter (*The Leader Letter*) about the Fear-Courage continuum that Pete was wrestling with. Here are the astute reflections of one reader, Ken Chisholm of Calgary, Alberta:

> *"My experiences have shown that fear is usually the underlying factor in a life of mediocrity and regrets. Fear of change, fear of being wrong, fear of the unknown, and fear of being successful — believe it or not.*

> *"Fear usually stems from surrounding oneself with negative people and naysayers who try hard to convince you that you won't succeed because they are more comfortable with you at or below their perceived level. If one is not strong enough to remove themselves from this influence they will soon believe this nonsense and incorporate it into their own self talk.*

Negative self talk can and will have a crippling effect if it is not recognized and corrected."

Like a black hole in space, the gravitational pull of fear can be an incredibly powerful force sucking us into its crushing depths. Canadian pollster Allan Gregg has found that a majority of people give in to worry and fear far too easily: "...of all the questions I have posed in polling throughout the years, perhaps my favorite is: 'If someone told you something was safe and someone else told you it was unsafe, which one would you believe?' A very small minority (10 percent) reported they would believe that this (undefined) something was safe, and 22 percent had the common sense to declare that it would depend on who was doing the telling and what they were talking about. But the vast majority — fully 68 percent — would accept the message of doom and gloom. That gives us a penetrating insight into the nature of fear and our reaction to the possibilities of exposure to risk."[87]

Fear does have a place in our lives. The motivational power

of fear can even be crucial to our survival. If we're physically attacked, fear can jolt us with the adrenalin and motivation we need for fight or flight. Fear is like fire. It can be a life-giving energy source or it can badly burn or destroy life.

Words of Warning: The Destructive Power of Fear

"The most destructive element in the human mind is fear. Fear creates aggressiveness....fear grows in darkness; if you think there's a bogeyman around, turn on the light... only when we are no longer afraid do we begin to live."

> Dorothy Thompson (1893–1961), American journalist

"Collective fear stimulates herd instinct, and tends to produce ferocity toward those who are not regarded as members of the herd."

> Bertrand Russell (1872–1970), British philosopher, logician, mathematician, and historian

"All of us are born with a set of instinctive fears — of falling, of the dark, of lobsters, of falling on lobsters in the dark, or speaking before a Rotary Club, and of the words 'Some Assembly Required.'"

> Dave Barry (1947–), American author and columnist

"Only fear can defeat life... it goes for your weakest spot, which it finds with unerring ease. It begins in your mind, always... nestles in your memory like a gangrene: it seeks to rot everything, even the words with which to speak of it... if your fear becomes a wordless darkness that you avoid, perhaps even manage to forget, you open yourself to further attacks of fear because you never truly fought the opponent who defeated you."[88]

> Yann Martel (1963–), Canadian author, Life of Pi, winner of Man Booker Prize

"I don't like being afraid. It scares me."

> Major Margaret J. "Hot Lips" Houlihan, fictional character in the American TV show M*A*S*H

"Nothing is more despicable than respect based on fear."

> Albert Camus (1913–1960), Algeria-born French author, philosopher, and Nobel Prize-winning journalist

www.JimClemmer.com

- A large selection of articles on Attitude and Outlook at http://www.jimclemmer.com/attitude.
- A selection of my writing and reader discussions on Attitude and Outlook from my **blog** and **monthly newsletter** at http://www.jimclemmer.com/newsletter/?cat=21.

Books

- Chapter Three, "Responsibility for Choices" of *Growing the Distance: Timeless Principles for Personal, Career, and Family Success.*
- Self-assessment, application ideas, and personal planning exercises in the "Responsibility for Choices" section of *Growing the Distance: Self-Study System.*
- For supervisors, managers, and executives – Chapter Three, "Responsibility for Choices" of *The Leader's Digest: Timeless Principles for Team and Organization Success.*
- Management team assessments, application ideas, and planning exercises in the "Responsibility for Choices" section of *The Leader's Digest: Practical Application Planner.*

V

No excuses for sinking thinking

WALLOW WORDS: THE TEMPTING TEN

"There is an eagle in me that wants to soar, and there is a hippopotamus in me that wants to wallow in the mud."

Carl Sandburg (1878–1967), American Historian,
Poet, and Novelist who won two Pulitzer Prizes

There are many reasons people succumb to the gravitational and magnetic draw of the dark forces that pull us down below the line to wallow in the swamp. These may include being unclear and unfocused; concentrating too much on yesterday or tomorrow and not living for today; getting our lives out of balance; not looking after our health; feeling inadequate; being too comfortable — for now. These could either be reasons for sliding into the swamp or signs that we're there.

This chapter is designed to help you do a wallow check. It's here to help you identify the negative forces exerting the strongest downward pull on you. *Warning*: This chapter is also intended to exorcise your excuses, infiltrate and stretch your comfort zone, and push you toward personal transformation so you can climb up the leadership stairs.

1. I AM NOT A BORN LEADER

"The most dangerous leadership myth is that leaders are born — that there is a genetic factor to leadership. This myth asserts that people simply either have certain charismatic qualities or not. That's nonsense; in fact, the opposite is true. Leaders are made rather than born."

Warren Bennis, Distinguished Professor of Business Administration and Founding Chairman of The Leadership Institute at the University of Southern California

Since I began studying, applying, and teaching leadership skills in 1975, I've believed to the core of my being that high performers are made, not born. Otherwise I would have given up long ago! When I was a sales trainer with Culligan Water Conditioning back in the seventies, I wrote a fictitious (and facetious) series of birth and death announcements poking fun at the popular misconception that we're either born talented or not. I revamped and revised the announcements and penned a passionate passage outlining my argument in the nineties when I wrote *Pathways*

to Performance: A Guide to Transforming Yourself, Your Team, and Your Organization. You can read it on our web site in my article "Leaders are Made, not Born." If we are not working hard to continually improve our leadership skills because we weren't "born with natural talent," then we are copping out, misinformed, or both.

There's now a body of solid research showing that leadership is much more about nurture than nature. A major study was reported in *Harvard Business Review*. Here are two key findings "....based on rigorous research (from over 100 leading scientists) that looked at exceptional performance using scientific methods that are verifiable and reproducible…in a variety of domains: surgery, acting, chess, writing, computer programming, ballet, music, aviation, firefighting, and many others":

- "Consistently and overwhelmingly, the evidence showed that experts are always made, not born." "…if you want to achieve top performance as a manager and a leader, you've got to forget the folklore about genius that makes many people think they cannot take a scientific approach to developing expertise."
- "…the journey to truly superior performance is neither for the faint of heart nor for the impatient. The development of genuine expertise requires struggle, sacrifice, and honest, often painful self-assessment."[89]

It's a dangerous excuse to believe that leaders are born not made. It takes you off the hook and gives you too easy an out from the difficult work of reframing your outlook and building your leadership skills.

Fortune magazine published an article entitled "Why Talent is Overrated" that addresses this critical self- and leadership-development question. The subtitle to the piece states, "The conventional wisdom about 'natural' talent is a myth. The real path to great performance is a matter of choice."

The article gives an example of two young men who started working together at Proctor & Gamble in the late seventies. They were unremarkable recruits who did not stand out in any way early in their careers. Writer Geoff Colvin quotes one of them as recalling, "We were voted the two guys probably least likely to succeed." Colvin goes on to write, "These two young men are of interest to us now for only one reason: They are Jeffrey Immelt and Steven Ballmer, who before age 50 would become CEOs of two of the world's most valuable corporations, General Electric and Microsoft. Contrary to what any reasonable person would have expected when they were new recruits, they reached the apex of corporate achievement."[90]

2. I DON'T HAVE THE AUTHORITY

"The most common way people give up their power is by thinking they don't have any."

Alice Malsenior Walker (1944–), feminist and American author who won the Pulitzer Prize for Fiction for her book The Color Purple

A central theme of my fictional story of Pete Leonard in *Moose on the Table®: A Novel Approach to Communications @ Work* was how he gave his power away by acting as if he was powerless. He and his team slowly learned how to be more and more helpless. It's a major problem I see time and again in my workshops and consulting work. The fascinating thing is how it runs up and down all levels of so many organizations.

A *Moose on the Table®* reader e-mailed me that she quite liked the book. She bitterly complained, though, about not being in a position of power or authority the way she thought Pete Leonard and the other characters were. She was partially right, in that this book was

directly applicable to those in supervisory or management roles. I targeted that group because they are the ones who so often disempower themselves; everyone else in the organization tends to see them as being more powerful than "the Petes" often see themselves as being. Pete's experiences were to provide a model for that group. They were also to provide a broader model for anyone wrestling with communication and courage.

Unfortunately, this reader fell into the trap of believing that power and authority come from position. I have long emphasized that *leadership is an action, not a position*. Leaders make it happen.

When we released *Moose on the Table®*, I delivered a national series of one-day *Breaking through the Bull* workshops. During one session, a participant blurted out, "Shouldn't senior management be addressing the moose issues and providing the leadership you've been discussing?" My answer was of course they should. But many don't.

That leaves you with three choices. 1. Live with the status quo (too many people who do that then jump on the Bitter Bus with lots of criticizing, condemning, and complaining). 2. Quit. 3. Provide strong leadership within your own team or area while practicing upward leadership. Too many people working under ineffective managers stay in unhappy situations, don't strengthen their own leadership, and choose to become victims of poor leadership from above. If you're one of them, pull yourself out of the muck and head toward the leadership stairs.

Now where did my attention wander off to?

3. I AM OVERLOADED AND OVERWHELMED

"Nowadays, people don't ask you how you are, they say, 'Are you busy?,' meaning, 'Are you well?' If someone actually does ask you how you are, the most cheerful answer, of course, is a robust 'Busy!' to which the person will reply, 'Good!' 'Busy' used to be a negative sort of word. It meant having no time for yourself, no leisure. 'No, I can't come out this weekend, I'm too busy.' Sorry about that, you poor stiff. Now, though, busyness is bullish. Conspicuous industriousness is the rule."[91]

Richard Stengel (1955–), Time magazine's 16th editor

One evening I was slowly eating my dinner with Heather. She waited and waited for me to finish and finally asked me to hurry up. I told her I was mindfully eating by savoring every bite of the delicious meal she had prepared. She told me to "savor faster."

"Fast savoring" is an apt oxymoron for our time. A few weeks later, the topic of frenzied busyness came up as I was writing a blog posting. A reader responded, "Today I am an employee that has been recently moved to a leadership role (overseeing/coordinating a team of five people). I was diagnosed with Attention Deficit Disorder (ADD) when I was in school and was medicated to deal with it. I had been working success-fully without medication for over five years. Since I have moved into my new role I have seen my ADD return."

She's not alone. We're in the midst of an epidemic deficit of focus and attention in our society. Ned Hallowell is a psychiatrist and the founder of the Hallowell Center for Cognitive and Emotional Health in Sudbury, Massachusetts. He began his career treating ADD

in kids. He's the author of 12 books, some of which deal with ADD in kids. They include *Driven to Distraction* and *CrazyBusy: Overstretched, Overbooked, and About to Snap. Strategies for Coping in a World Gone ADD.* He also published an article in *Harvard Business Review* entitled "Overloaded Circuits: Why Smart People Underperform."

Hallowell has found that managers and professionals in the 21st century suffer from a newly recognized neurological phenomenon that he calls Attention Deficit Trait, or ADT. "It isn't an illness; it's purely a response to the hyperkinetic environment in which we live. But it has become epidemic in today's organizations….people with ADT have difficulty stay-ing organized, setting priori-ties, and managing time, and they feel a constant low level of panic and guilt."[92] He reports that the number of patients with ADT coming into his clin-ical practice has mushroomed tenfold in a decade.

Hallowell finds that the benefits of multitasking are illusionary and a big part of the ADT problem. Many people believe that younger generations raised in an environment of juggling multiple technologies at once are better at multitasking. Numerous studies have shown that to be completely false. Stress research has found that shifting attention every few minutes to respond to incoming electronic messages increases levels of cortisol (a stress hormone), which decreases memory function. Studies by Glenn Wilson, a psychologist at King's College London, showed an average IQ loss of 10 points among 1,100 frequent electronic communicators who were flipping back and forth between tasks, conversations, and their electronic messages.

I don't know about you, but I can't afford to lose 10 IQ points! So I shut off all of those notifications. By point of comparison, marijuana smoking causes only a four-point IQ drop. You'd have to miss a whole night of sleep in order to get to the ten-point drop caused by the technology distractions measured in the study.[93]

What big, brown, hairy creature?

4. I AM AVOIDING THE MOOSE-ON-THE-TABLE

"Many times, often with the best of intentions, people at work decide it's more productive to remain silent about their differences than to air them. But as new research....shows, silencing doesn't smooth things over or make people more productive. It merely pushes differences beneath the surface and can set in motion powerfully destructive forces."[94]

Leslie Perlow and Stephanie Williams, "Is Silence Killing Your Company?" Harvard Business Review

Like the elephant in the room, the moose-on-the-table is a metaphor representing problems or issues that aren't being addressed. The moose stands on the meeting room table while everyone does his or her best to pretend it's not there.

Moose live in swampy areas. They thrive below the line in our homes and organizations. Here's a quiz to assess the extent of moose problems in your workplace. Many of the examples apply equally at home.

Rate the following examples for signs of a big or little moose on the loose:

1 No Moose	2	3 A Little Moose	4	5 A Big Moose
1	2	3	4	5
1	2	3	4	5
1	2	3	4	5
1	2	3	4	5
1	2	3	4	5
1	2	3	4	5
1	2	3	4	5
1	2	3	4	5
1	2	3	4	5

1. The real discussion happens privately after our meetings.
2. People appear to agree to a group plan of action then go off and do their own thing.
3. Personal accountability and commitments are avoided and project deadlines are routinely missed.
4. A few vocal people dominate conversations and cut off dissenting opinions before they've been fully expressed.
5. Once the team leader gives his or her opinion, everyone else agrees or remains silent.
6. Finding someone to blame for a problem or spending time explaining why it occurred is more common than trying to understand the underlying root cause.
7. Surprises happen as simmering problems erupt into major issues.
8. People feel overwhelmed by too many priorities and conflicting messages about what's important.
9. We keep adding to our to-do lists and rarely spend time agreeing on what to stop doing.

Rate the following examples for signs of a big or little moose on the loose:

1	2	3	4	5
No Moose		A Little Moose		A Big Moose

10. There's turf protecting, simmering conflict, and people taking potshots at other departments/groups.

1	2	3	4	5

11. Time is wasted discussing unimportant details while bigger priorities and key decisions don't get enough attention.

1	2	3	4	5

12. We don't debate all sides of important issues and avoid touchy or politically sensitive topics.

1	2	3	4	5

Scoring:

SCORE OF 12-24: *No Bull*

Congratulations! You don't seem to have a moose problem. Ask other members of your team to go to www.mooseonthetable.com and take this quiz to see if they agree with you.

SCORE OF 25-30: *Moose Crossing Ahead*

It looks like there may be a few baby moose lingering in the halls. But don't panic. You should be able to herd them into an elevator and send them on their way.

SCORE OF 31-36: *Watch Your Step*

Moose are starting to pop up all over the place. It's getting crowded. If you don't keep an eye on where you're going, you may find yourself ankle deep in moose droppings.

SCORE OF 37-45: *Time for Action*

It looks like your organization is becoming a perfect habitat for moose. If you don't start hunting them soon, you may find the place overrun before you know it!

SCORE OF 46-60: *Face the Big Bull*

It's moose-hunting season! You have big moose on the table, under the table, and snacking in the lunch room. It's time for courageous leadership.

The Boy and the Filberts

"A boy put his hand into a pitcher full of filberts. He grasped as many as he could possibly hold. But when he tried to pull out his hand he was prevented from doing so by the neck of the pitcher. Unwilling to lose his filberts, and yet unable to withdraw his hand, he burst into tears and bitterly lamented his disappointment. A bystander said to him, 'Be satisfied with half the quantity and you will readily draw out your hand.'"

Do not attempt too much at once.

Aesop Fables

5. THE BAD NEWS IS GETTING ME DOWN

"The more important and widespread reason for the media's pessimism is that journalists have every incentive to accentuate the negative. Media organizations prize skepticism: Pollyannas are frowned upon; Cassandras get promoted. Even Chicken Littles are tolerated, as long as they come up with hot copy. Why? Bad news sells. Just as a forecast like HURRICANE THREATENS WASHINGTON D.C. gets more viewers than one saying STORM MAY PETER OUT OVER CAROLINAS, a headline that says IS THIS ANOTHER DEPRESSION? will sell more papers than RECESSION MAY NOT BE SO BAD."[95]

Rob Norton, *"The Recession Lovers' Club,"* Fortune

"Nattering nabobs of negativism" was a phrase originally coined by speechwriter William Safire for U.S. vice-president Spiro Agnew to describe the media who opposed the Nixon administration's policies. It's an apt phrase for the professional pessimists in the media, especially during turbulent times. What's considered "news" or reported as "reality" is overwhelmingly what's wrong, not what's right.

"If it bleeds it leads" is an old truism in the newspaper business. Random acts of violence are reported in great detail while random acts of kindness go largely unnoticed. Unemployment rates are reported as reaching 8, 10, or 12 percent rather than employment rates of 88, 90, or 92 percent. A 40 percent chance of rain is what we're told rather than a 60 percent chance of sunshine.

Will Rogers (1879–1935), humorist, and social commentator, once said, "I hope we never live to see the day when a thing is as bad as some of our newspapers make it." In his book *Is Progress Speeding Up?: Our Multiplying Multitudes of Blessings*, successful investor Sir John Templeton writes, "…people today, on the average, are better fed, better clothed, better housed, and better educated than at any previous time. Fewer and fewer people live under the weight of tyranny. In most parts of the world, people are enjoying longer, healthier, more fulfilling lives."[96]

Daily, I read a few news web sites and weekly, I scan about a dozen others. I am interested in what's happening around the world. I also look for research and examples to file in my electronic database — and use in books such as this one. Through years of training and habit-building, I've worked hard to see beyond the sensationally negative headlines for all the good and the positive progress we're making.

Will I ever get enough?

6. I WANT MORE STUFF

"Few men own their own property. The property owns them."

Colonel Robert Green Ingersoll (1833–1899), Civil War veteran, American political leader, and orator

Research is clearly showing just how much truth is found in the cliché "money doesn't buy happiness." The explosion in happiness studies since 2000 shows that despite dramatically rising standards of living in Western countries, levels of happiness have not increased. In some cases, they've actually decreased as stress levels from persuing "the good life" increased. One study surveyed respondents on the Forbes 400 list of richest Americans and the Masai people of East Africa. They found almost equal satisfaction reported by both groups. The Masai have no electricity or running water and live in dung huts. The researchers concluded, "…economic development and personal income must not account for the happiness they are so often linked to."[97]

All of this research is finally causing a major reassessment of whether economic growth should be the ultimate goal of society. Grinding poverty — especially if others around us are doing much better — causes unhappiness. But once our physical and financial needs are adequately met, loving relationships, good health, helping others, spiritual beliefs, community involvement, a clean environment, connections to nature, living our values and strengths, fulfilling work, and a sense of positive contribution to our world are much stronger happiness factors.

How do you define wealth?

How Much Land Does a Man Need?

Russian novelist Leo Tolstoy wrote a short story of this title about Pahom, a peasant farmer who was given a chance for free land. Carrying a spade, he had to pace out the land in a large circuit starting from any spot. He was to dig holes to indicate corners or boundaries. But "before the sun sets you must return to the place you started from."

Pahom eagerly started out at the crack of dawn. Most of the land was very fertile. It was filled with hills, dales, streams, and marshes. He traced a circuitous route around the very best land. Late in the day he realized that his greed had taken him very far from his starting point. So he began a desperate race with the setting sun to get back to where he started.

With his distant finish line in sight and the sun fast disappearing, Pahom ran the last mile at top speed. He collapsed at his starting point just as the sun set. He made it! His servant came to help him up. He found blood flowing from Pahom's mouth. "Pahom was dead… his servant picked up the spade and dug a grave long enough for Pahom to lie in, and buried him in it. Six feet from his head to his heels was all he needed."[98]

7. I AM TOO BUSY TO LEARN

"The illiterate of the 21st century will not be those who cannot read and write, but those who cannot learn, unlearn, and relearn."

Alvin Toffler (1928–), American writer and futurist

I've spent decades listening to people explain that they just don't have time for personal learning or investing in training and organizational development. As they get busier, they have even less time for learning. As they have less time for learning, they need to work harder because the tools and skills they are using get ever duller. As they work harder and faster using old ideas, methods, and approaches, there's even less time to learn how to be more effective. This spiral leads down the slippery slope into — you guessed it — the swamp.

I contrast this all-too-common "victim" approach with the highly effective people, teams, and organizations I've been privileged to work with.

They have reversed the vicious busy circle into a virtuous circle of continuous growth and development, leading to ever more effectiveness which leads to less crazy-busyness and more time to learn. Here's how Barry Chow, a Client who's built a highly successful business in Calgary, Alberta, puts it:

> *"'I don't have time to learn,' is actually equivalent to 'I don't have time to improve.' This is poison to both our professional development and to our own fulfillment as individuals.*
>
> *"'Learning' is sometimes easy to dismiss, whereas 'improving' is an unarguably desirable goal that leaves no wiggle-room*

for procrastination. Learning isn't just some necessary evil that we were finished with after our schooling, but a

lifelong process that is indispensable to our continuing growth and improvement as human beings."

What if they figure out I'm not perfect?

8. I CAN'T LET ANYONE SEE MY MISTAKES

"Aim for success, not perfection. Never give up your right to be wrong, because then you will lose the ability to learn new things and move forward with your life. Remember that fear always lurks behind perfectionism. Confronting your fears and allowing yourself the right to be human can, paradoxically, make yourself a happier and more productive person."

David M. Burns, American psychiatrist

Progress — especially in turbulent times — means climbing stairs we've never been on before. For leaders on the grow, failing-our-way-to-success, experimenting with trial and error is exciting. As revered Nobel prize-winning physicist Albert Einstein observed, "If we knew what it was we were doing, it would not be called research, would it?" For wallowers, mistakes are threatening. Fear is often the dark force behind their search for the right black-and-white answer. Below-the-line fear is what causes people to expect perfection from themselves and others. Of course, that never happens. There is no such thing as perfection.

Here's where language and actions can again expose underlying values and expectations. Wallowers will speak of mistakes, disasters, failures, blunders, and punishment as they search for the guilty to hang from a lamppost. Leaders will speak of setbacks, feedback, testing, good tries, and what can be learned from the experience.

My old colleague Jack Zenger, co-founder of Zenger Miller (now part of AchieveGlobal), and Joseph Folkman report on leadership studies showing that successful leaders made the same number of mistakes as unsuccessful ones did. But the former openly acknowledged what happened, tried to fix it, learned from the experience, and moved on. The latter hid their mistakes, did not alert colleagues or take steps to rectify the problem, and brooded about the problem for years. "Our research confirms that the inability to learn from mistakes is the single biggest cause of failure."[99]

Wallow Hollow: Why should I ever let them off the hook?

9. I CARRY ANGER AND RESENTMENT

"Holding on to anger is like grasping a hot coal with the intention of throwing it at someone else — you are the one who gets burned."

Buddha

Anger and resentment are normal emotions when we've been hurt by someone else or experience a traumatic event. They may even be vital first steps in our healing process. Wallowing in these negative emotions, though, is our biggest danger. Turning anger into hate is especially deadly. Hate is like acid; it eats up the container that holds it. In many ways, it's a prolonged form of suicide. It's like sending a letter bomb to a person we hate, only to have the package returned to us. Failing to recognize our own silently ticking box, we open it and unleash all that destruction on ourselves. Hate is the ultimate "return to sender." It always comes back to haunt you.

The effects of anger, hostility, and being unforgiving have been studied in depth and with some surprising results. The research shows, for example, that — contrary to popular belief — we should not try to express our anger to get rid of it. That intensifies the emotion and makes it worse. It's also been found that harboring bitter feelings of betrayal increases stress and blood pressure and can dramatically multiply our chances of a stroke or heart attack.

The Bee and Jupiter

"A bee from Mount Hymettus, the queen of the hive, ascended to Olympus to present Jupiter some honey fresh from her combs. Jupiter, delighted with the offering of honey, promised to give whatever she should ask. She therefore besought him, saying, 'Give me, I pray thee, a sting, that if any mortal shall approach to take my honey, I may kill him.' Jupiter was much displeased, for he loved the race of man, but could not refuse the request because of his promise. He thus answered the bee: 'You shall have your request, but it will be at the peril of your own life. For if you use your sting, it shall remain in the wound you make, and then you will die from the loss of it.'"[100]

Evil wishes, like chickens, come home to roost.

Aesop's Fables

10. WE DON'T COMMUNICATE

"The way we communicate with others and with ourselves ultimately determines the quality of our lives."

Anthony Robbins (1960–), American self-help
writer and professional speaker

It's ironic but in today's age of instantaneous communication and technologies that have made us a global village, communication breakdowns are the single biggest complaint I hear from our Clients. It's a complex issue with both cause and effect tightly intertwined. In many cases, people don't have the skills to address tough issues with each other. And so they do it poorly and raise defensiveness in the other person, or stir up conflict that can get personal and quite vicious. Many times people are afraid to speak up because they have seen others who have be ostracized, nudged off the promotion track, ignored, or punished with the least desirable assignments.

Adding to the noise of communication issues is the technology overload. Lots of people confuse "communicating" with "dumping information" through copious electronic messages or, God forbid, more PowerPoint slides. This in reality reduces meaningful two-way communication. Everyone is scrambling to frantically clear in-boxes or fitfully make it through yet another meeting. There is no time for thoughtful and difficult conversations. Quantity is confused with quality.

As if that weren't enough, when the organization's structure is badly designed and the processes or methods for moving information, work flow, products, or customers through it are flawed, all kinds of errors, rework, waste, and frustration build up. People will often look at the resultant mess and say, "We need more communication around here." In fact, they probably need less, but they need it to be better! In these cases, communication problems are a symptom of underlying problems with processes, systems, or organizational structure.

The key question is, "What are you doing to help remedy things?" You're either part of the problem or part of the solution. There is no middle ground. You can ride the Bitter Bus below the line and complain about "them" or "nobody ever tells me anything." Or you can build your communication skills, go get the information you need, connect with others, and identify the moose-on-the-table. You can act like a leader.

TO KEEP YOU GROWING

Here's where you can find more of my material on the topics covered in this chapter.

www.JimClemmer.com

- Peruse a few dozen articles on Personal Growth and Continuous Improvement at http://www.jimclemmer.com/growth.
- A selection of my writing and reader discussions on Personal Growth and Continuous Improvement from my **blog** and **monthly newsletter** at http://www.jimclemmer.com/newsletter/?cat=15.

Books

- Chapter Three, "Responsibility for Choices" of *Growing the Distance: Timeless Principles for Personal, Career, and Family Success.*
- Chapter Three, "Responsibility for Choices" of *The Leader's Digest: Timeless Principles for Team and Organization Success.*
- Go to www.mooseonthetable.com for video clips explaining each chapter and an overview of the book.

PART
FOUR

Lead to
Succeed

VI

WE ALL NEED TO LEAD: LEADERSHIP IS ACTION, NOT A POSITION

"We can't control the wind, but we can adjust our sails."

North American proverb

The Wallower curses the wind.
The Follower waits for it to change.
The Leader adjusts the sails.

To wallow is to say, "They are doing it to us again." To follow is to wait for "somebody to do something." To lead is to move forward with the conviction "if it is to be, it's up to me." Leading means taking initiative. Leading is getting up and showing the way. Leading employs persuasion rather than the power of position. Like the best navigators in the days of the ancient mariners, leading means figuring out how to capitalize on — or overcome — the conditions nature or life throws at us.

Many people think narrowly of leadership as an appointed role. In our organizations and institutions, we do need clarity around roles and responsibilities. It does need to be evident where "the buck stops" and who's in charge.

But the action of leading — living above the line, seeing new possibilities, encouraging and supporting, reframing, harnessing the winds of change to grow forward, and overcoming helplessness with hopefulness — needs to be broadly shared by everyone everywhere, regardless of formal roles or positions. The scope of leadership might be determined by roles, but the actions of leadership are determined by approach. To thrive above the line in turbulent or calm times, we all need to be leaders in every aspect of our lives. True leadership is defined by what we do, not the position we hold. Leadership should be a verb, not a noun.

The Winds of Fate

"One ship drives east and another
   drives west,
With the self-same winds that blow,
'Tis the set of the sails
And not the gales
That tell them the way to go.

Like the winds of the sea are the
   winds of fate,
As we voyage along through life,
'Tis the set of the soul
That decides its goal
And not the calm or the strife."

Ella Wheeler Wilcox (1850–1919),
American author and poet

Leaders don't wait, they initiate. Leading ourselves and others up the leadership stairs is the route to good health, happiness, and success. We need "leaderful" teams and organizations to inspire everyone upward to higher performance and results. "We are going to do something" is the language of success. "Something must be done" is the language of failure.

Wise Words on Acting like a Leader

"Our only chance for contributing is to quit waiting and wondering and do something. We serve ourselves and others best when we do not wait. Initiate, with the organization and all involved people in mind. No, we are not in charge but we can act. No, we are not formally designated leaders. But we can lead."[101]

Geoffrey M. Bellman, Getting Things Done When You Are Not in Charge

"Everybody can lead at every level; there are no excuses. It doesn't matter if you're on the front line or the top line... do you excite and motivate people? Do you bring excellence and vision...everybody should be good at leading, whatever their level in the hierarchy."[102]

Michael Useem, director of Wharton's Center for Leadership and Change Management at the University of Pennsylvania and author of many articles and books on leadership

"Self-help must precede help from others. Even for making certain of help from heaven, one has to help oneself. "

Morarji Ranchhodji Desai (1896–1995), Prime Minister of India

"'There is a set of skills and capabilities that are useful at the lowest levels; you exert it through your peers and in team settings,' Wharton management professor Anne Cummings says. Leadership in the lower ranks can involve everything from prioritizing tasks and managing time to getting people to accomplish goals and resolving conflicts. Such commonplace actions are important because they help an organization at any level meet its goals."[103]

"Why Everyone in an Enterprise Can — and Should — Be a Leader," Special Report on Leadership in collaboration with McKinsey Quarterly

"Few will have the greatness to bend history itself but each one of us can work to change a small portion of events, and in the total of all those acts will be written the history of this generation."

John Fitzgerald "Jack" Kennedy (1917– 1963), 35th President of the United States

MY GREAT KIDNEY ADVENTURE

"As a physician, I have had many experiences over the years that have led me to conclude that the world of clinical medicine is truly bizarre and unpredictable, a territory where almost anything is possible. Most of my colleagues, I feel, agree, for almost all physicians possess a lavish laundry list of strange happenings unexplainable by normal science. A tally of these events would demonstrate, I am convinced, that medical science has not only not had the last word, it has hardly had the first on how the world works — especially when the mind is involved."[104]

Dr. Larry Dossey, Recovering the Soul:
A Scientific and Spiritual Search

Thirty years after I discovered the stairway to a new way of thinking, leading to a whole new reality, I faced my first significant physical test of applying these principles. This turbulent time of personal adversity deeply challenged me to move from the study and belief of the mind/body/spirit connection to its practical application.

In August of 2005, our family doctor continued his tradition of "fishing expeditions" during my annual physical examination. He had me undergo an abdominal ultrasound of all my vital organs. The ultrasound showed a mass on my right kidney. I was immediately referred to an urologist. He specialized in kidney cancer and told me that 90 percent of kidney masses are malignant tumors. He scheduled an operation to remove my kidney. He also scheduled a CT scan in three weeks to get a better look at the tumor in preparation for the operation. This scan would also verify if it was the tumor he suspected or a more harmless cyst.

Heather and I were in shock. Over the years, I'd become very health conscious. With regular exercise, a healthy diet, adequate sleep, teaching and continuously building my optimistic skills, I was in great physical and mental shape. My mind-body connection had proved to be very strong. I had missed only two days of work, with stomach pains during a very stressful time in my life, in 33 years.

I did take a few therapeutic visits below the line to Pity City over the next few days with some anger, resentment, and "why me?" thrown in. Since the CT scan was in three weeks Heather and I decided to get back above the line and intensely apply every mind/body/spirit principle we knew. We had 21 days until K Day (Kidney Day). Thus began my Great Kidney Adventure….to be continued with how-to steps in Part Five.

EMOTIONAL INTELLIGENCE: THE LEADING EDGE

Emotional Intelligence: *"A form of social intelligence that involves the ability to monitor one's own and others' feelings and emotions, to discriminate among them, and to use this information to guide one's thinking and action."*

Peter Salovey, Professor of Psychology and Management and Dean of Yale College at Yale University, and John Mayer, psychologist at the University of New Hampshire, first coined and defined the term "Emotional Intelligence" in 1990

In most organizations — and much of society — we have deep-rooted beliefs that smart people are more successful. We often recruit the "brightest and best" candidates for our schools and organizations through screens like Scholastic Aptitude Testing (SAT scores) and other indicators of analytical and reasoning abilities. We tend to value, envy, promote, and take pride in people who are gifted, talented, accomplished, clever, brainy, logical, intellectual, deep thinking, scientific, or have strong technical expertise — especially if they're our kids!

A minimum level of IQ is needed to function independently in society. Every profession or job also demands a minimum level of reasoning, logic, and problem-solving abilities. But numerous studies are now showing that, contrary to popular beliefs, IQ levels explain only 4 percent or at the most 10 to 25 percent of the differences between success and failure. Some studies have actually shown an inverse relationship between IQ and success: The brightest individuals in the peer group were the least successful.

Many psychologists and researchers saw serious limitations with IQ testing and were looking for other factors to explain job performance and life success. The foundations for "non-intellective" or "multiple intelligences" — social and emotional intelligences — were then laid, as far back as the late thirties. These other forms of intelligence take into account our perception or cognitive framework, explanatory style, range of reality, consciousness, energy vibrations, balance of optimism or pessimism, hopelessness or hopefulness, fear and worry, wallowing, following, or leading ... they are all outflows of our emotional state. Feelings and emotions are a major part of what it is to be human. They influence us as much as or more than any IQ we could possibly measure.

In the early nineties, Daniel Goleman was a science writer for *The New York Times*, covering brain and behavior research. He had been trained as a psychologist at Harvard where he worked with David McClelland — one of a growing group of researchers concerned with how little traditional tests of cognitive intelligence (IQ) told us about what it takes to be successful in life.

After years of following the emerging research on Emotional Intelligence, in 1995 Goleman published his first in a series of books on the topic. *Emotional Intelligence: Why It Can Matter More Than IQ* became an international bestseller, introducing this field squarely into the mainstream. The book and high-profile articles by Goleman and his colleagues in publications like *Harvard Business Review* ignited an explosion in Emotional Intelligence research, tools, training, and other applications.

Having spent decades trying to better understand, apply, explain, and teach the "soft" skills of personal growth and leadership, I was very excited to come across the groundbreaking

Emotional Intelligence research in 1997. Since then, I've been an avid collector of any findings. I continue to marvel at the ways in which it brings rigor, discipline, and empirical research to the fuzzy and subjective topic of personal, team, and organizational leadership. It's a great way to think logically about feelings — to go through the head to get at issues of the heart. The Emotional Intelligence Competency Framework is a strong leadership model that clearly shows what it takes to live and lead above the line.

The Power of Emotional Intelligence

"This emotional task of the leader is primal — that is, first — in two senses: It is both the original and the most important act of leadership....in the modern organization, this primordial emotional task — though by now largely invisible — remains foremost among the many jobs of leadership: driving the collective emotions in a positive direction and clearing the smog created by toxic emotions. This task applies to leadership everywhere, from the boardroom to the shop floor... if people's emotions are pushed toward the range of enthusiasm, performance can soar; if people are driven toward rancor and anxiety, they will be thrown off stride."[105]

Primal Leadership: Realizing the Power of Emotional Intelligence, *Daniel Goleman, Richard Boyatzis, and Annie McKee*

- "90 percent of our believability and credibility may be based on EQ not IQ."[106]

- "A study of Harvard graduates in the fields of law, medicine, teaching, and business found that scores on entrance exams — a surrogate for IQ — had zero or negative correlation with their eventual career success."[107]

- "If the partner (in an international accounting firm) had significant strengths in the self-management competencies, he or she added 78 percent more incremental profit than did partners without those strengths. Likewise, the added profits for partners with strengths in social skills were 110 percent greater, and those with strengths in the self-management competencies added a whopping 390 percent incremental profit."[108]

- "After supervisors in a manufacturing plant received training in emotional competencies, lost-time accidents were reduced by 50%, formal grievances were reduced from an average of 15 per year to 3 per year, and the plant exceeded productivity goals."[109]

- "...even among scientists and those in technical professions analytic thinking ranks third, after the ability to influence and the drive to achieve. Brilliance alone will not propel a scientist to the top unless she also has the ability to influence and persuade others, and the inner discipline to strive for challenging goals."[110]

- "....analysis of myriad jobs found that emotional competence makes up about two thirds of the ingredients of star performance in general, but for outstanding leaders emotional competencies — as opposed to technical or cognitive cues — make up 80 to 100 percent of those listed by companies themselves as crucial for success."[111]

EMOTIONAL COMPETENCE FRAMEWORK

"Rule your feelings, lest your feelings rule you."

Publilius Syrus, 1st century Latin writer of maxims. He was brought as a slave to Italy, but by his wit and talent won the favor of his master, who freed and educated him.[112]

Formed in 1996, The Consortium for Research on Emotional Intelligence in Organizations (www.eiconsortium.org) is co-chaired by EI pioneers Daniel Goleman and Cary Cherniss. The group draws from academia, government, the corporate sector, and private consulting. This organization and its core members distilled research on Emotional Intelligence into the Emotional Competence Framework. It provides a highly useful roadmap of the inner (personal) and outer (social) dimensions of living and leading above the line.

PERSONAL COMPETENCE

Self-Awareness
- *Emotional Awareness*: Recognizing one's emotions and their effects.
- *Accurate Self-Assessment*: Knowing one's strengths and limits.
- *Self-Confidence*: Sureness about one's self-worth and capabilities.

Self-Regulation
- *Self-Control*: Managing disruptive emotions and impulses.
- *Trustworthiness*: Maintaining standards of honesty and integrity.

- *Conscientiousness*: Taking responsibility for personal performance.
- *Adaptability*: Flexibility in handling change.
- *Innovativeness*: Being comfortable with and open to novel ideas and new information.

Self-Motivation
- *Achievement Drive*: Striving to improve or meet a standard of excellence.
- *Commitment*: Aligning with the goals of the group or organization.
- *Initiative*: Readiness to act on opportunities.
- *Optimism*: Persistence in pursuing goals despite obstacles and setbacks.

SOCIAL COMPETENCE

Social Awareness
- *Empathy*: Sensing others' feelings and perspectives, and taking an active interest in their concerns.
- *Service Orientation*: Anticipating, recognizing, and meeting customers' needs.
- *Developing Others*: Sensing what others need in order to develop, and bolstering their abilities.
- *Leveraging Diversity*: Cultivating opportunities through diverse people.
- *Political Awareness*: Reading a group's emotional currents and power relationships.

Social Skills
- *Influence*: Wielding effective tactics for persuasion.
- *Communication*: Sending clear and convincing messages.
- *Leadership*: Inspiring and guiding groups and people.
- *Change Catalyst*: Initiating or managing change.
- *Conflict Management*: Negotiating and resolving disagreements.
- *Building Bonds*: Nurturing instrumental relationships.
- *Collaboration and Cooperation*: Working with others toward shared goals.
- *Team Capabilities*: Creating group synergy in pursuing collective goals.

TO KEEP YOU GROWING

Here's where you can find more of my material on the topics covered in this chapter.

www.JimClemmer.com

- Review articles on Emotional Intelligence at http://www.jimclemmer.com/EQ.
- A selection of my writing and reader discussions on Emotional Intelligence from my **blog** and **monthly newsletter** at http://www.jimclemmer.com/newsletter/?cat=33.

Books

- Chapter Four, "Self-Leadership: It All Starts with You" of *Pathways to Performance: A Guide to Transforming Yourself, Your Team, and Your Organization.*
- "Emotional Intelligence" pages 155–157 of *Growing the Distance: Timeless Principles for Personal, Career, and Family Success.*
- "Soft Skills, Hard Results" in *Growing the Distance: Self-Study System.*
- "Soft Skills, Hard Results" pages 24–28 of *The Leader's Digest: Timeless Principles for Team and Organization Success.*
- The fictional character, Pete Leonard, in *Moose on the Table®: A Novel Approach to Communications @ Work* at first avoided his leadership responsibilities but eventually increased his Emotional Intelligence to lead above the line. Go to www.mooseonthetable.com for video clips explaining each chapter and an overview of the book.

VII

No matter who you are or what you do, you can L-evate yourself.

FOR THE L OF IT: LIVING AND LEADING ABOVE THE LINE

"I am only one; but still I am one. I cannot do everything, but still I can do something; I will not refuse to do the something I can do."

Helen Keller (1880–1968), American author, political activist, lecturer, and the first deaf-blind person to earn a Bachelor of Arts degree

When someone is appointed to a leadership role, he or she is often called a leader. But many people in leadership roles aren't leaders. They might be vice-presidents, teachers, CEOs, managers, administrators, department heads, directors, or even "snoopervisors" — but they're not leaders.

Too many appointed leaders sit on the line and wait rather than taking the initiative and making things happen. They follow someone else's lead. Some slip down below the line and wallow in hopelessness and pessimism — which they'll often call "being realistic." In both cases, these are "leaders" by their position. But their actions show they aren't leading.

This chapter builds on the premise that we all need to be leaders regardless of our organizational, family or community position. In this chapter, we'll take a quick tour of what living and leading above the line — leadership action — looks like. The rest of the book will outline a broad series of options and steps you can take to thrive above the line — through all the change and adversity life may throw at you.

Livened by the Law of Attraction.

POSSIBILITY THINKING: SPREADING HOPE AND OPTIMISM

"The problems of the world cannot possibly be solved by skeptics or cynics whose horizons are limited by the obvious realities. We need people who can dream of things that never were."

John Keats (1795–1821), English poet

Leaders make us hopeful. Whether leading ourselves, our families, our teams, organizations, or countries, when times are darkest true leadership shines brightest. Leaders don't sugarcoat or avoid facing tough problems head-on (the moose-on-the-table). Strong leaders inspire their co-workers, teams, associates, friends, or loved ones to be hopeful by focusing on what could be as a counterbalance to what is. Leaders know how powerful and self-fulfilling the Law of Attraction truly is. They set up positive magnetic fields that attract the behaviors, circumstances, and events that ultimately lead to success.

Business advisor and coach Harry Hudson and cultural anthropologist and management consultant Barbara Perry are authors of *Putting Hope to Work*. In an article entitled "The Leaders from Hope," they report:

"…work connected to the positive-psychology movement has made hope discussable in new ways. Hope has been shown to be the key ingredient of resilience in survivors of traumas ranging from prison camps to natural disasters. Many studies have shown that people who score higher on measures of hope also cope better with injuries, diseases, and physical pain; perform better in school; and prove more competitive in sports."[113]

Lift others above the line.

ENCOURAGING, SUPPORTING, AND HELPING

"Note how good you feel after you have encouraged someone else. No other argument is necessary to suggest that we never miss the opportunity to give encouragement."

George Burton Adams (1851–1925),
American educator and historian

When our daughter Vanessa was 20 years old, I came home one day to find her beaming and proudly displaying a new necklace she was just given as a thank-you gift. It seems I'd just missed her visitor, Jeremy, who had dropped by to express his appreciation for Vanessa's "tough friendship" when the two of them were in a precollege preparatory course a year earlier. Jeremy was struggling with drug and alcohol problems. Throughout the school year, Vanessa altered between scolding him and reinforcing just what potential she believed he had. She told him about Alcoholics Anonymous and encouraged him to attend. When he told her he was planning to move to Western Canada to get away from the negative influence of his family and friends, she strongly encouraged him to follow his heart.

Now he was back in Kitchener-Waterloo visiting family and friends. He went out of his way to thank Vanessa for setting him on the path to recovery and life renewal. He had been steadily attending AA meetings and was pulling his life together. Jeremy was so inspired by the changes in his life that he planned to become an addictions counselor in Vancouver. This experience gave Vanessa and me a chance to reflect on the power of encouraging, supporting, and helping others. Leaders build others up and look for ways to challenge or coach them out of the swamp and onto their leadership stairway.

The Gift

An African girl presented a Christmas gift to her teacher. When the teacher unwrapped the gift, she found a beautiful seashell. Asked where the child could have found it, she told her teacher those unique shells come only from a special faraway beach. The teacher was very touched and remarked, "You shouldn't have gone so far for a gift for me." The girl looked at her, smiled, and replied, "The long walk is part of the gift."

Author Unknown

Learn that less is more.

REFLECTING, RENEWING, AND REFOCUSING

"Successful leaders strive to become more reflective. That's paradoxical given that today's business culture celebrates action over hesitancy. Americans in particular admire leaders who break new ground, transform industries, and smash glass ceilings. Given this overemphasis on doing, perhaps it's not surprising that many of the fallen leaders I studied appeared to have a strikingly impoverished sense of self. Though they often know how to read others brilliantly, they remain curiously oblivious to many of their own tendencies that expose them to risk."[14]

Roderick M. Kramer, social psychologist and professor of organizational behavior at Stanford University

I once sat through a scarily high-energy presentation given by an academic specializing in knowledge management. He poured out an overwhelming array of statistics showing that the world's knowledge was growing at mind-blowing rates. The gist of his presentation was that we need to retrain our brains to absorb more and more information, more and more quickly. His goal seemed to be to bombard us into using his knowledge management approaches so we could cram more stuff in our craniums.

This is dead wrong. He was peddling dangerous misconceptions leading to high stress, attention deficit disorder, and unhappiness. In times of dramatic, discombobulating, light-speed change, we need to step back to step ahead. We need to slow down to increase our speed.

The growing mass of research on time effectiveness, strategic focus, our increasing volume of electronic messages, happiness, dealing with stress, relationships, coaching … the list is endless … clearly shows us that less is more. Paradoxically, we get more done, build stronger teams, and increase personal and organizational effectiveness by stepping back regularly to assess our progress, savor our successes, celebrate achievements, and set new priorities.

L-ectrify your energy.

THREE QUESTIONS AT OUR LEADERSHIP CORE

"The leader who is centered and grounded can work with erratic people and critical group situations without harm. Being centered means having the ability to recover one's balance, even in the midst of action. A centered person is not subject to passing whims or sudden excitements…the centered and grounded leader has stability and a sense of self."[115]

John Heider, The Tao of Leadership: Lao Tzu's Tao Te Ching Adapted for a New Age

My energy force field vibrates from the core of who I am. A team or organization's energy and culture vibrate from its collective core. That core is formed by what I or we focus on, and the context of our lives or team and environment. I have long called this central leadership principle Focus and Context. It's at the hub of our Leadership Wheel. This is the frame that *Growing the Distance: Timeless Principles for Personal, Career, and Family Success, The Leader's Digest: Timeless Principles for Team and Organization Success*, related workbooks, and our training programs are built around.

Our Focus and Context core heavily influences our perceptions, explanatory style, Range of Reality, and positive or negative energy levels. I've been caught up in lots of debates over the years on definitions of organizational vision, values, and purpose/mission. Whatever they might be called, the key questions forming our Focus and Context are:

- Where are we going?
- What do we believe in?
- Why do we exist?

> **Imagery and visualization have incredible self-fulfilling power than science is only beginning to understand.**

Where we are going involves the use of imagery and visualization. This has an incredible self-fulfilling power and vibrational magnetic energy that new research frontiers like quantum mechanics and mind-body medicine are only beginning to understand. What we believe in defines our deep-seated values or attitudes that establish the frames or filters we wear to determine as good or bad whatever is happening to us. These values also guide our behaviors. Why we exist takes us to the fundamental issues of finding or defining deeper meaning for our teams, our organizations, and our own time on this earth.

SMARTENING UP: BOOSTING EMOTIONAL INTELLIGENCE

"That's an important lesson from neuroscience: Because our behavior creates and develops neural networks, we are not necessarily prisoners of our genes and our early childhood experiences. Leaders can change if... they are ready to put in the effort."[116]

Daniel Goleman and Richard Boyatzis, "Social Intelligence and the Biology of Leadership"

An early debate in the emerging Emotional Intelligence research was whether our EQ, like IQ, is fixed once we hit adulthood. The debate is over and the verdict is in: like building leadership or other forms of expertise, we can improve our EQ at any time in our lives. In one study at Case Western Reserve University, Master of Business Administration (MBA.) students were given Emotional Intelligence training (not a normal part of most very analytical MBA programs). In follow-up studies many years after the program, some students had raised their EQ scores 40 percent![117]

Richard Boyatzis, professor and chair of the department of organizational behavior at Case Western Reserve University, says it's not a lack of ability to change but an issue of motivation. He likens this leadership development issue to treatments for alcoholism, drug addiction, and weight loss. "They all require the desire to change. More subtly, they all require a positive, rather than a negative, motivation. You have to want to change."[118]

Many EI coaches have found that self-awareness is a

key first step on the stairway to boosting our Emotional Intelligence. Howard Book, associate professor in the department of psychiatry at the University of Toronto, suggests, "One simple way to measure your self-awareness is to ask a trusted friend or colleague to draw up a list of your strengths and weaknesses while you do the same. It can be an uncomfortable exercise, but the bigger the gap between your list and your helper's, the more work you probably have to do."[119]

> Self-awareness is a key first step on the stairway to boosting our Emotional Intelligence.

Leading Example on Developing Self-Awareness

"One of the techniques I have found most useful in gaining deeper self-awareness is meditation. In 1975, my wife dragged me, kicking and screaming, to a weekend course in Transcendental Meditation. I have meditated 20 minutes, twice a day, ever since. Meditation makes me calmer, more focused, and better able to discern what's really important. Leaders, by the very nature of their positions, are under extreme pressure to keep up with the many voices clamoring for their attention. Indeed, many leaders lose their way. It is only through a deep self-awareness that you can find your inner voice and listen to it."[120]

William George, former chairman and CEO of Medtronic, a world leader in chronic-disease treatment

Limber up your tolerance.

LIVING IN THE LEADERSHIP GRAY ZONE

"There ain't no answer. There ain't gonna be any answer. There never has been an answer. There's the answer!"

Gertrude Stein (1874–1946), American expatriate
writer, poet, playwright, and feminist

When our son Chris was home from university to celebrate his 22nd birthday, he and I had a conversation about how much more complex, nuanced, and interesting the world has become for him than when he was a teenager. During his teenage years, the world, and most of the people he encountered in it, could be easily divided into right and wrong, stupid and smart, good and bad, cool and not cool, and so on. With his interest in politics, we had many ideological debates about the social and political issues of the day. He had strong beliefs and clear answers for just about every situation. I often argued both sides of an issue — even the side I didn't believe in — to try to help him understand that it wasn't that black and white.

Chris's major in first-year university was "political science." He had failed to find the humor in me calling "political science" an oxymoron. At the time of this discussion, though, he was in his third year and had to write papers arguing both sides of issues, even presenting the opposite side to his own belief. He had become more tolerant and understanding of the world's subtleties and complexities. In other words, he had grown up.

There are clearly times when we do need to take a stand and draw a firm line between what we see as right and wrong or moral and immoral. Hiding behind ambiguity or waffling on our position can be a sign of weakness and a genuine lack of leadership. But the capacity to live in the gray zone between black and white is a sign of maturity. A great deal of destruction and disaster in organizations, relationships, families, religions, and throughout societies comes from the intolerance and inflexibility of immature "leaders" who believe there are clear right and wrong answers to just about every situation. Their harsh and judgmental positions usually come from a place of fear.

Mature leaders can live with not having clear answers and letting situations unfurl. They seek to understand with a more accepting position that comes from a place of compassion and love.

Let go and let yourself grow.

STRATEGIC WORRY VERSUS WALLOW WORRY

""Relax — it will all work out' simply isn't always true. We have to make things work out for ourselves... defensive pessimism is a strategy that helps us to work through our anxious thoughts rather than denying them, so that we may achieve our goals."[121]

Julie Norem, Associate Professor of Psychology at Wellesley College, The Positive Power of Negative Thinking: Using Defensive Pessimism to Harness Anxiety and Perform at Your Peak

Pick up a cup of water or coffee and estimate how heavy it is. Now hold it straight out sideways at shoulder height. How much heavier does it feel? What if you hold it that way for five minutes? How about an hour? Imagine if you tried to hold it that way for a day. In the unlikely event you could, your arm and shoulder would need serious medical attention.

Pessimism and negative explanatory styles cause us to hold on to past wrongs, problems, and stress for far too long. The longer we hold on, the heavier those burdens become. As we hold on, we fantasize and magnify the issue far beyond its original size. We make the proverbial mountain out of a molehill. As Mark Twain quipped, "I am an old man and have known a great many troubles, but most of them never happened." That's wallow worry. It's deadly to our health, happiness, relationships, performance, and just about everything else in our lives.

Nature equipped us to worry as a way of preparing for danger. We do need stress for success. Strategic worry — I've also heard it called strategic pessimism — involves anticipating problems and proactively avoiding, minimizing, or overcoming them. It's the kind of prescient worry that leads us to take constructive action. I very much want the pilots of the planes I fly on to practice strategic worry before and during every flight.

> *"I am an old man and have known a great many troubles, but most of them never happened."*
> Mark Twain

COURAGEOUS LEADERSHIP: STRETCHING OUR COMFORT ZONE

"Courage is doing what you are afraid to do. There can be no courage unless you're scared."

Eddie Rickenbacker (1890–1973), World War One American fighter ace and Medal of Honor recipient, early race car driver, and founder of Eastern Airlines

Courage is the foundation of leadership. The Greek philosopher Aristotle believed courage was the foundation of all human virtues, because it made the others possible. Our progress up the leadership stairway is strongly determined by the extent of our courage. Are we continually stretching our comfort zone? Are we ready to address personal and professional obstacles blocking our growth? To live and lead above the line we must listen to our inner voice and act on the courage of our convictions.

Do we have courageous conversations? Do we seek feedback that we don't want to hear? Are we open to opposing views or approaches? Do we speak up? What about our courage to address team or organization issues that are impeding progress? It's much easier to be quiet and just go along. And the silence can say it all.

One of the liveliest discussions we've had among readers of my blog and newsletter, *The Leader Letter*, has been about courageous leadership. Ken Chisholm of Calgary, Alberta reflected, "I have gone into many meetings, conversations, situations with some fear and trepidation only to come out with the highest feeling of accomplishment. To face your fears without compromising your values is one of life's most rewarding experiences." Another reader, Diane Cappel of Freeport, Texas wrote, "Throughout my life I have found that not stepping up and sharing my beliefs or challenging the status quo were the times I suffered the most. When fear held me hostage I felt more pain from not living up to my standards than I ever did by standing up for my convictions. Time and again I have witnessed good people who let their fear of what might happen if they stand up for what they believe keep them bound, silent, and miserable. Fear makes slaves, courage enables freedom."

Look up and lead.

UPWARD LEADERSHIP

"You may be thinking, 'But someday I will be in charge of the committee (or agency or division or team) and I will change things!' Well, think again. That's akin to getting married with the plan to start changing your spouse immediately after the ceremony. My research says that does not work very well…it is too easy for us to attribute power to a position that we have yet to hold, or that others hold, and to diminish the power we currently have."[122]

Geoffrey Bellman, Getting Things Done
When You Are Not in Charge

It's easy to sail a ship when the sea is calm. It's easy to look like a brilliant investor in a bull market. And it's easy to be positive and stay above the line when we have an optimistic, supportive, and highly effective boss. What takes courage, skill, and Emotional Intelligence is upward leadership, when we have a weak or a bad boss. You may have a boss who needs a surge protector to buffer his or her mouth from emotional outbursts. Or a wind sock outside his or her office to gauge abrupt changes in direction.

The lousier your boss or those higher up in your organization are at setting priorities, the better you and your team must be at stepping into the breach. You may need a daily, weekly, or monthly process to reset your goals and priorities as conditions and demands change.

Try to better understand the bigger picture that your boss and others above you in the organization are operating within. Do you know what keeps them awake at night?

What are their key goals and priorities? Don't wait to be told — find out. Don't wait for your boss or someone else to open the door. The handle is on the inside.

Dealing with a boss is what clearly separates the wallowers and followers from the leaders. Wallowers will complain bitterly that their boss doesn't communicate and give them the information they need. Followers will passively wait for the information and perhaps understand that their boss is busy, disorganized, or not getting the information from above. Leaders will ask questions, quietly persist or gently insist until they get the information they need. This takes skill, this takes initiative, and this takes courage. This is leadership.

> *Leaders will ask questions, quietly persist or gently insist until they get the information they need.*

MASTERING OR MANAGED BY YOUR TECHNOLOGY?

"I don't blame technology. I blame the way we use it. You need a system to confront what I call screen-sucking — literally being constantly drawn to a new hit of information... you don't have to answer every e-mail the minute you get it. And there is no reason that you have to deal immediately with every interruption that comes up.... People don't realize how much they've given up control and allowed their boundaries to be much too permeable."[123]

Edward Hallowell, former professor at Harvard
Medical School and now director of the Center for
Cognitive and Emotional Health

Electronic tools are incredible. They can enhance communications, build relationships, and increase time effectiveness. Electronic tools can also replace true communication with information overload, damage relationships, and overwhelm our day. Yes, electronic tools are vital and valuable, but they can also become vampires sucking our vital time and energy. Is it time you put them down or put on the screen saver and saved yourself? Let's see.

Measuring Your E-Beast

How true are the following statements:

	1 Not True	2	3 Somewhat True	4	5 Very True
1. I am notified whenever a new electronic message is sent to me.	1	2	3	4	5
2. Electronic messages are consuming more and more of my day and reducing personal communication.	1	2	3	4	5
3. I use my electronic in-box(es) as a holding area or To-Do list and feel overwhelmed by all the messages there.	1	2	3	4	5
4. An endless stream of electronic messages interrupts my work all day long and leaves me with little thinking/planning time.	1	2	3	4	5
5. I often check my electronic messages while talking with someone or in a meeting.	1	2	3	4	5
6. I spend too much time checking and answering electronic messages in off hours and my spouse/family finds this frustrating and intrusive.	1	2	3	4	5
7. I am caught in electronic discussions that circle back and forth instead of picking up the phone, calling a meeting, or going to someone's office.	1	2	3	4	5
8. I have not developed electronic protocols/ground rules or similar agreements with my team, peers, and boss.	1	2	3	4	5
9. Many electronic messages I get have irrelevant subject lines, unclear expectations or reasons for me getting them, long conversation strings to decipher, or are copied to inappropriate people.	1	2	3	4	5
10. I generally jump right into my daily electronic messages without prioritizing and putting strict limits on the time I've allocated to dealing with them.	1	2	3	4	5

	1	2	3	4	5
	Not True		Somewhat True		Very True
11. Sometimes I'll send an electronic message rather than have a difficult conversation with individuals or groups.	1	2	3	4	5
12. I haven't managed expectations on how quickly internal people can expect an electronic response from me.	1	2	3	4	5

Scoring:

- **45 points or higher** — Godzilla the E-Beast is on a destructive path through your life. You've disempowered yourself and you're wallowing below the line in the high-stress swamp of information overload. You need to make major changes to get above the line.

- **30–44 points** — The E-Beast you've been feeding is holding you on or below the line and blocking you from taking control of your life. Strengthen your Emotional Intelligence to better balance using information technology and verbal communications.

- **16–29 points** — Your E-Beast is small and weak. Keep leading and using verbal communications to keep it in check.

- **15 points or lower** — Congratulations! Your E-Beast is tame, trained, and helping you stay above the line. Continue climbing those leadership stairs and help others learn to leverage technology as effectively as you do.

Highly effective leaders manage IT tools to leverage their effectiveness and improve their communications. They don't let the tools manage them.

BOUNCING BACK ABOVE THE LINE

"In Japan, there is a common good luck charm called a Daruma Doll. It is named after a Buddhist monk who, according to legend, sat so long in meditation that his arms and legs disappeared. The Daruma Doll is egg shaped with a heavy, rounded bottom. When you knock it over it always stands back up. Lucky people are similar to the Daruma Doll. It is not that they never encounter ill fortune, but rather, when bad luck happens, lucky people are able to stand straight back up."[124]

Richard Wiseman, The Luck Factor:
Change Your Luck and Change your Life

Life is full of problems, setbacks, and loss. That's unavoidable. Misery, though, is optional. Failure can be a learning experience or it can knock us into the swamp where we wallow, whine, and waste away. It all depends on how we frame the reality of our situation. Wallowers accentuate the negative and make the setback permanent, pervasive, and personal.

Leaders get knocked down but like the Daruma Doll, get right back up. Through an optimistic explanatory style, leaders figure out how to climb back from losses or negative changes. Leaders are hardy and help to inspire and build resilient teams. Leaders and their teams often fail their way to success. Leaders see the defeat as temporary, isolated, and specific to a set of circumstances.

Defeat

No one is beat till he quits,
No one is through till he stops,
No matter how hard Failure hits,
No matter how often he drops,
A fellow's not down till he lies,
In the dust and refuses to rise.

Fate can slam him and bang him around,
And batter his frame till he's sore,
But she never can say that he's downed
While he bobs up serenely for more.
A fellow's not dead till he dies,
Nor beat till no longer he tries.[125]

Edgar A. Guest (1881–1959), American poet known
as the People's Poet, A Heap O' Livin'

TO KEEP YOU GROWING   Here's where you can find more of my material on the topics covered in this chapter.

www.JimClemmer.com

- Review articles on Management versus Leadership at http://www.jimclemmer.com/leadership.
- A selection of my writing and reader discussions on Management versus Leadership from my **blog** and **monthly newsletter** at http://www.jimclemmer.com/newsletter/?cat=27.

Books

- Chapter Three, "The High-Performance Balance: Managing Things, Leading People" of *Pathways to Performance: A Guide to Transforming Yourself, Your Team, and Your Organization.*
- Chapter One, "The Way of the Leader" in *Growing the Distance: Timeless Principles for Personal, Career, and Family Success.*
- Chapter One, "Leaders Make the Difference" in *The Leader's Digest: Timeless Principles for Team and Organization Success.*
- Management team assessment in "The Performance Balance" section of *The Leader's Digest: Practical Application Planner.*
- The fictional character, Pete Leonard, in *Moose on the Table®: A Novel Approach to Communications @ Work* learned how to use the approaches outlined in this chapter to turn his job and life around. Go to www.mooseonthetable.com for video clips explaining each chapter and an overview of the book.

PART
FIVE

Step Up
to a New
Reality

VIII

If you can't see it, you can't be it;
viewing it is the first step to doing it.

MAGNETIC ATTRACTION: VIBRATING THE STRINGS OF YOUR FORCE FIELD

"The action of Mind plants that nucleus which, if allowed to grow undisturbed, will eventually attract to itself all the conditions necessary for its manifestation in outward visible form...[126] *The whole livingness of Life consists in receiving or in radiating forth the vibrations produced by the law of attraction... they become desires. Desire is therefore the mind seeking to manifest itself in some form which as yet exists only in its thought."*[127]

Thomas Troward (1847–1916), English world religions
researcher/synthesizer, author, and lecturer whose works influenced
the New Thought Movement and mystic Christianity

I first came across the Law of Attraction in 1974. It fundamentally shifted my reality and changed my life. As outlined in Chapter Two, there's a rapidly growing body of scientific research, such as quantum mechanics and string theory, helping us to understand this incredibly powerful magnetic force. Whenever we think about the future, whether the next few days or longer term, we're visualizing or imagining potential scenarios, actions, and outcomes. The *vital* question is whether we're visualizing a future that's mostly above or mostly below the line. What we focus on energizes our personal force field.

Since fear and pessimism are so easy to give in to, we seem to most easily visualize what we don't want, and then bring that into being. That's what worry is. Turning around years of negative conditioning and bad habits so we can learn to vividly see what we do want takes hard work and forming new thought patterns. We need to change our automatic explanatory styles and cognitive framework. A powerful and proven approach is reversing the downward spiral of negative, self-defeating thoughts with positively charged images visualizing what circumstances, people, or events we want to attract to our lives.

We're all different, so there is no universal, one-approach-fits-all way to enhance our positive visualization. You need to learn how to use the imagery techniques that work best for you. There is a proliferation of books, video/audio recordings, articles, and web sites on how to tap into this very powerful life force. On the book site Amazon.com, for instance, search "imagery" or "visualization." On the web, search "imagery techniques," "visualization techniques," "guided imagery," and similar phrases.

You'll be in awe of the science you find. For example, "psychoneuroimmunology" is a burgeoning new medical field that is bringing together psychology, neurosciences, immunology, pharmacology, psychiatry, behavioral medicine, infectious diseases, and rheumatology. What a world we're growing toward!

IMAGERY AND MY GREAT KIDNEY ADVENTURE

"Mind-Body Medicine focuses on the interactions between mind and body and the powerful ways in which emotional, mental, social and spiritual factors can directly affect health...these techniques include self-awareness, relaxation, meditation, exercise, diet, biofeedback, visual imagery, self-hypnosis and group support....the techniques exert their effect on the hypothalamus, the switching station in the brain, which exercises control over the autonomic nervous system... The scientific literature on these approaches is now rich and robust....these techniques have been demonstrated to create beneficial changes in many of the body's physiologic responses (including blood pressure, stress hormone levels, pain response and immune functioning) and to make a significant clinical difference in conditions as diverse as hypertension, HIV, cancer, chronic pain, and insomnia as well as anxiety, depression, and post-traumatic stress disorder."[128]

James S. Gordon, Harvard-educated psychiatrist, founder and Director of The Center for Mind-Body Medicine, a Clinical Professor in the Departments of Psychiatry and Family Medicine at Georgetown Medical School, and past Chairman of the White House Commission on Complementary and Alternative Medicine Policy

On page 113, I outlined the shock Heather and I experienced when I was told I probably had kidney cancer: a 90 percent chance. After some "therapeutic wallowing," we decided to get back above the line and use the three weeks until my scheduled CT scan to activate my mind-body connection and try to get "the placebo effect" to kick in. We began an extensive and intensive series of imagery exercises, reaching out to others, prayer, meditation, energy healing activities; you name it, we probably did it.

Here are just a few examples of the imagery or visualizations we used:

• Heather developed a "Think Pink" campaign (as in a pink and healthy kidney) based on a Pink Panther site she found full of logos and drawings. She e-mailed me one per day along with purchasing a stuffed Pink Panther, feathered pink flamingo, and glass "Raphael the Healer" angel for my desk.

• I reviewed the video, cards, and books on water crystals from Dr. Emoto (see page 44) and used this as the basis for water and word images:

− We purchased pillow cases with "Peace," "Love," "Health" and "Prosperity" printed on them.

− I put small Post-it-Notes™ with words like "Love," "Health," "Gratitude," "Thank You," and "Family" on my water glass, and wrote the same words on water bottles I was drinking.

− I thanked and blessed water in all forms and as I slowly drank it I visualized pure, healing, energy-filled water molecules flowing throughout my body into every cell.

− I thanked water for nurturing and cleansing me as I urinated and visualized tiny bits of the kidney mass being flushed out of me.

− During walking meditation on our treadmill as a cooldown to my running session, I imagined standing under a waterfall with the clean, pure, loving water coursing through, in, and around my body, totally restoring each cell to perfect balance.

— After the workout and meditation, I thanked water in the shower and continued to visualize my body being cleansed from all non-divine material inside and out, and being drained away into the river, lakes, and oceans to be purified and recycled as pure, life-giving rain.

- Periodically during the day or at night while going to sleep, I visualized the power of my body's white blood cells washing away the dark mass on my kidney.

- During a sunny day, I would expose my right side to the sun while taking deep relaxing breaths and visualizing the spiritual light chasing away all interior shadows.

- I drew a heart with a sun in it symbolizing love and light on my side over my kidney; I also drew a sun with a heart inside.

- I visualized — and Heather and I joked about — seeing ourselves at age one hundred surrounded by loving children, grandchildren, and great-grandchildren.

This is just a portion of what we did during the three weeks leading up to my scheduled CT scan, which was expected to basically "confirm" the diagnosis of a 90 percent chance of kidney cancer. The week after the CT scan, we went to the urologist for the results. He looked at the file and said he hoped I hadn't cancelled any speaking engagements around the day of my scheduled operation. He then beamed and announced that the scan showed all I had was a benign cyst.

The best words I could imagine were written on the note he sent back to his receptionist: "Cancel Operating Room." Those words were as magical as "I Do" or "It's a boy" or "It's a girl."

We'll never know whether we actually changed whatever was on my kidney. Did we activate the powerful mind-body connection? What we clearly did do was use the powerful force of visualization and imagery to channel our anxiety and stress toward positive action. That alone allowed me to relax, stay mostly above the line, and sleep well.

Visualization Tips and Techniques

- At least once a year, describe what your ideal life would look like if things were going extremely well three to five years from now. Outline your perfect job. Envision your ideal family life. See yourself helping to build whatever communities you're now part of. Visualize a strong and secure financial situation. Imagine your preferred social circle. Feel an even stronger connection to your philosophical or spiritual beliefs. See your optimum health or physical condition. Include your spouse or "significant other" as a joint exercise; two visualizations are probably better than one.

- Use photos, drawings, or symbols to paint the pictures of your preferred future. Assemble a collage of these from magazines, web sites, sketches, or clip art that represent what you want to attain, the kind of person you want to be, your ideal role or position, your preferred family or social life, the kind of community you want to help build, your physical well-being, and so on. Keep your collage in a prominent place to keep you focused on where you're going.

- If you have an illness or physical condition, research and apply the ongoing advances in the emerging fields of Mind-Body Medicine and Psychoneuroimmunology.

- Begin with the end in mind. As you undertake a big task, bring about a major personal change, or embark on a long project, continually visualize your success. Surround yourself with images, symbols, pictures, positive reinforcement, encouraging people, and uplifting messages.

- Counteract the stress and anxiety feeding your mind a steady stream of negative, fear-filled images with a continual stream of positive images of your preferred outcomes. Use visualization or imagery to picture yourself brilliantly giving a presentation, confronting an issue, reaching an agreement, or mastering whatever you might be anxious about doing.

- Develop a "dream list" to help find the core of your deepest and truest inner desires and visions. Brainstorm every dream, desire, or goal that pops into your mind. Once the list is fairly complete, you can sift through it to look for patterns or clusters. This doesn't have to happen overnight; you might want to keep a running list for a while.

www.JimClemmer.com

- Articles on Personal Vision, Values and Purpose at http://www.jimclemmer.com/values.
- A selection of my writing and reader discussions on Personal Vision, Values, and Purpose from my **blog** and **monthly newsletter** at http://www.jimclemmer.com/newsletter/?cat=19.

Books

- Chapter Seven, "Picturing Your Preferred Future" of *Pathways to Performance: A Guide to Transforming Yourself, Your Team, and Your Organization.*
- Chapter Two, "Focus and Context" of *Growing the Distance: Timeless Principles for Personal, Career, and Family Success.*
- A guided visualization exercise (I talk you through it) and other personal imagery application ideas in the Focus and Context section of the *Growing the Distance: Self-Study System.*
- For supervisors, managers, and executives — Chapter Two, "Focus and Context" of *The Leader's Digest: Timeless Principles for Team and Organization Success.*
- Management team assessments, application ideas, and planning exercises in the "Focus and Context" section of *The Leader's Digest: Practical Application Planner.*

IX

IN THE ZONE: ALIGNING PERSONAL VALUES, STRENGTHS, AND PURPOSE

"Our personalities, we may discover, are a veritable patchwork quilt of bits and pieces picked up along the superhighway of life from friends, relatives, even magazines and movies, then sewn together into a single artificial cloak we wear each day and call 'I.' When this realization begins to dawn we start to ask, "Where's the real me?"[129]

Harry Moody and David Carroll, The Five Stages of the Soul: Charting the Spiritual Passages That Shape Our Lives

I grew up during the sixties and early seventies in the small farming community of Milverton, Ontario, in Perth County just north of Stratford. Arden Barker was a farmer, local politician, and well-known community builder. His wife Helen was also very active in the community and wrote a weekly newspaper column filled with her wit, experiences, observations, and philosophies. Helen was highly engaged in life and made everyone she met feel like she got up that day just to make you feel important.

Helen died in 2005. A tribute to her life was held at the Milverton arena and community centre, because no other building in the area could hold the large crowd that attended. Helen was a strong supporter of my writing, so her daughter Brenda asked to read a piece I'd written in *Growing the Distance: Timeless Principles for Personal, Career, and Family Success*. It was an old Barker family story that reinforced appreciating what we've accomplished rather than focusing on what we lack. During the celebration of Helen's life, Brenda and other speakers reviewed all that Helen had endured: the sudden death of her son Tom at age 19; Arden's premature death at 59; adopting and raising two abused teenage girls later in Helen's life; her years of battling cancer, and other disasters and losses. To her last day, Helen remained thankful for all that life gave her, positive, and concerned with others and the community. It was a unique opportunity to reflect on the life and legacy of a strong above-the-line leader.

Events like these are times to reflect on what's really important. Happiness research confirms what most of us intuitively know: living a purposeful, meaningful life aligned around our personal values and strengths is critical to enjoying a successful journey for the short time we're traveling on this earth.

Core Values: Tips and Techniques

Effective leaders have a strong sense of self. They are comfortable in their own skin. Strong leaders have high levels of Emotional Intelligence. A cornerstone of EI is self-awareness.

- Brainstorm a list of everything you value. This might include career, family, learning, achievement, sports, wealth, socializing, inner peace, happiness, status, awards or credentials, autonomy, love, expertise, cuisine, artistic expression, home, making a difference, authenticity, friendships, travel, adventure, spirituality; list everything that is important to you. Cluster all your similar values until you have three to five groups. Put a heading or title on each group. Write a sentence or short paragraph defining each cluster. Examples of cluster headings could be Personal Growth, Achievement, Social Life, Well-Being, Family, or Financial Security. These are your core values. They are at the hub of your being.

- Look more deeply at your values. Are they truly your beliefs or are they what other people or institutions have said you should care about? Are they your internal "bone-deep" beliefs or

an external "should" value? We often don't recognize a lifetime of conditioning that has left us with other people's belief systems. We need to replace any "should" values with our own.

- Practice meditation or solitude to quiet all your external chatter and listen to your voice within. Where is your heart telling you to go? Your deepest happiness and fulfillment is down that path.

- Take a look at your schedule for the next few weeks or months. As you look ahead, are you energized and excited or enervated and stressed? How aligned are your schedule and your values? Do your personal and professional activities line up to your values in the right proportions or has life slipped out of balance? Don't allow today's urgencies to crowd out what's really important in your life.

- Contribute to authentic conversations in an authentic workplace. Speak the truth as you see it, with diplomacy and tact. Help others (especially your peers and those above you) to address the moose-on-the-table.

Oh no, paid for what I know, or off to work I grow.

THE MEANING OF YOUR WORK

"Except for the financially desperate, people do not work for money alone. What also fuels their passion for work is a larger sense of purpose or passion. Given the opportunity, people gravitate to what gives them meaning, to what engages to the fullest their commitment, talent, energy, and skill. And that can mean changing jobs to get a better fit with what matters to us."[130]

Daniel Goleman, Working with Emotional Intelligence

Any job can become a career or calling, and any career or calling can become a job. A scientist, physician, or pastor may have initially felt called. But if he or she finds work has become drudgery, it's now a job. An hourly production worker or hospitality server may have started in a job and progressed to feeling a calling to make better products, happier people, or the world a little better place. He or she now has a career or even, yes, a calling.

Job

- A means to some other end.
- Provides financial support.
- Not much else expected from the work.
- Little loyalty or emotional commitment ("work is a four-letter word").
- Move on if a better job, usually with more money or benefits, comes along.

Career

- Mark achievements through income, advancements, power, or prestige.
- Usually involves ongoing training and development.
- Focus on a particular profession/trade/skill set.
- Often certified, licensed, or credentialed.
- "Topping out" — little further advancement — can cause midlife crisis or big career changes.
- A significant source of personal identity.

Calling

- Fulfilling a sense of purpose and making a meaningful difference.
- Contributing to a greater good that's bigger than you — a sense of service.
- Aligned with your values and strengths.
- Being is more important than doing or having.
- Following an inner voice to what you're called to do.
- Higher income is a bonus, but not a key driver.
- Promotions to greater responsibility may expand impact or might be an unwelcome distraction from the work at the center of the calling.
- Time often flies by.

Which of these three defines most clearly why you work?

Which one would you like your work to be?

STRENGTHS-BASED LIVING

"Authentic happiness comes from identifying and cultivating your most fundamental strengths and using them every day in work, love, play, and parenting."[31]

Martin Seligman, Authentic Happiness: Using the New Positive Psychology to Realize Your Potential for Lasting Fulfillment

The nonprofit VIA Institute on Character (www.viastrengths. org) was founded to create a scientifically rigorous classification of character strengths and a way of measuring them. The VIA (Values In Action) survey is based on 24 universal character strengths defining what's best about people. The VIA Survey is the result of a three-year effort involving 55 noted social scientists. Approximately one million people have taken the VIA Survey on Character Strengths. The 24 character strengths are clustered into six groups:

1. **Wisdom and Knowledge** — creativity, curiosity, judgment and open-mindedness, love of learning, and perspective.

2. **Courage** — bravery, persistence, honesty, and zest.

3. **Humanity** — capacity to love and be loved, kindness, and social intelligence.

4. **Justice** — teamwork, fairness, and leadership.

5. **Temperance** — forgiveness and mercy, modesty and humility, prudence, and self-regulation.

6. **Transcendence** — appreciation of beauty and excellence, gratitude, hope, humor, and religiousness and spirituality.

Aligning Values and Strengths: Tips and Techniques

- Complete tests like VIA Character Strengths, the Kolbe Index, Myers-Briggs Type Indicator, Gallup's Strength Finder Profile, Social Styles, and so on to determine your personal style and how you can maximize your preferences and strengths while working effectively with varying styles among co-workers or team members.

- You can manually brainstorm a list of all of your strengths. In addition to those listed above in the VIA Survey, your list might also include Emotional Intelligence, technical aptitude, service orientation, training/teaching, speaking, writing, self-discipline, helping others, visionary or strategic thinker, or trustworthiness. List any quality or strength you feel you have to some degree. Now cluster similar strengths until you have three to five groups. Put a heading or title on each group. Cluster headings might include Persuasive Communications, Leading Others, Personal Growth, Achievement Drive, or Generosity. Write a sentence or short paragraph defining each cluster. These are your core strengths. They are your energy source.

- If you're in a management position but your work isn't energizing you so you can energize and lead others, you have four choices: (1) Do nothing and wish for your "fairy job mother" to appear, poof!, and straighten out your life. (2) Get out of a leadership role so you stop dragging others down to your low energy level. (3) Realign your work with your values and strengths. (4) Figure out what your ideal job is and go find or create it.

- Develop hobbies or special interests that play to your values, strengths, and passions.

- Don't focus on your weaknesses unless they become "fatal flaws" that seriously hold you back. Instead, concentrate on your strengths and how to align all aspects of your life with them.

- If you're a sumo wrestler, don't waste time trying to be a ballerina. We can't teach frogs to fly. Don't allow others to "should" on you by making you feel guilty about your weaknesses (as long as they are not fatal flaws) and telling you what you should do. Do what aligns with your values, strengths, and purpose.

www.JimClemmer.com

- Articles on Personal Vision, Values, and Purpose at http://www.jimclemmer.com/values.
- A selection of my writing and reader discussions on Personal Vision, Values, and Purpose from my **blog** and **monthly newsletter** at http://www.jimclemmer.com/newsletter/?cat=19.

Books

- Chapter Eight, "Principles" and Chapter Nine "Purpose" of *Pathways to Performance: A Guide to Transforming Yourself, Your Team, and Your Organization.*
- Chapter Two, "Focus and Context" of *Growing the Distance: Timeless Principles for Personal, Career, and Family Success.*
- "Clarifying My Core Values," "Why Do I Exist?" "Determining my Strengths," and "Checking My Work Alignment," along with dozens of Personal Application Ideas in *Growing the Distance: Self-Study System.*
- The fictional character, Pete Leonard, in *Moose on the Table®: A Novel Approach to Communications @ Work*, wrestles with his values and searches for his courage to lead above the line. Go to www.mooseonthetable.com for video clips explaining each chapter and an overview of the book.
- For supervisors, managers, and executives – Chapter Two, "Focus and Context" of *The Leader's Digest: Timeless Principles for Team and Organization Success.*
- Management team assessments, application ideas, and planning exercises in the "Focus and Context" section of *The Leader's Digest: Practical Application Planner.*

X

To feel great, be grateful;
to be grating, be hateful.

REWIRE YOUR BRAIN WITH AFFIRMATIONS, REFRAMING, AND GRATITUDE

"Before I was paralyzed there were 10,000 things I could do. Now there are 9,000. I can either dwell on the 1,000 I've lost or focus on the 9,000 I have left."[132]

W. Mitchell, *survivor of a blazing motorcycle accident and a paralyzing plane crash, founding chairman of a $65-million company, two-term mayor and congressional nominee, Hall of Fame professional speaker, radio host, television personality, and author of* It's Not What Happens to You, It's What You Do About It

Roman emperor Marcus Aurelius once observed, "Our life is what our thoughts make it." If our thoughts are constantly below the line, we'll not only live in Pity City, we'll start to run the place. What we repeatedly think or tell ourselves become powerful instructions that reach deep into our subconscious. In essence, we hypnotize ourselves. No, we may not jump on stage and do the chicken dance when we hear a trigger word, but we will perform ridiculous acts of mindlessness, thanks to self-conditioning.

You need a better mantra, man!

AFFIRMATIONS: MIND PATROL

"Autosuggestion is an instrument we possess at birth, and with which we play unconsciously all our life… autosuggestion is nothing but (self) hypnotism… it can wound or even kill you if you handle it imprudently…it can on the contrary save your life when you employ it consciously…every thought entirely filling our mind becomes true for us and tends to transform itself into action."[133]

Self-Mastery Through Conscious Autosuggestion, *Emile Coué (1857–1926), French psychologist and pharmacist*

An affirmation is a statement, belief, or thought that we repeat over and over again. It becomes a powerful mantra that changes our brain patterns, sets our explanatory filters, and programs our subconscious. Affirmations direct our behaviors and habits.

They also power our magnetic energy fields to attract the corresponding people, events or circumstances to us. When the positive or negative outcome occurs, we can say, "I knew it! That's exactly what I expected to happen."

Negative Affirmation	Positive Affirmation
I am so stupid.	I am getting better.
I never do this right.	I am mastering this skill.
I am trying to lose weight.	I am healthy and fit.
Life's a bitch and then you die.	I am grateful for what I have.
I am always tired or sick.	I radiate energy and health.

Positive Affirmations: Tips and Techniques

- Stop yourself from saying things like, "I am too old to change," "That's just the way I am," or "There's nothing I can do."

- Identify those habits or characteristics you'd most like to change. Your list could include fitness, wealth, energy, friendships, discipline, eating, or self-control. You might refer to your values, character strengths on page 154, or the Emotional Intelligence Framework on pages 118–119.

- Now develop a series of positive affirmations as if it's already happening. For example, "I am ...," "I love to ...," or "I can ... ."

- Post your affirmative statements where you'll see them every day. You could use them as screensavers, or put Post-it-Notes™ in your work space, bathroom mirror, car, wallet, purse, briefcase, or day planner.

- Change and rotate your affirmations or move them around every few days so you keep noticing them.

- You can also post quotations, truisms, or inspirational sayings to energize and reinforce the changes you're making.

REFRAMING: LEADING EXPLANATIONS

"The key to disputing your own pessimistic thoughts is to first recognize them and then to treat them as if they were uttered by an external person, a rival whose mission in life was to make you miserable."[34]

Martin Seligman, Authentic Happiness: Using the New Positive Psychology to Realize Your Potential for Lasting Fulfillment

Cognitive Behavioral Therapy (CBT) has made tremendous strides in helping people with pessimistic explanatory styles become much more optimistic. This involves teaching how to dispute below-the-line thought through self-argument, weighing objective evidence, exploring more desirable alternatives, "decatastrophizing" the long-term implications, and challenging the usefulness of dwelling on that negative belief/view.

Consider finding a trained CBT psychologist to coach your reframing efforts. It could alter your reality. It really could change your world.

Reframing Tips and Techniques

- Don't generalize or judge. Instead of generalizing — "life's unfair" — you might more specifically say, "This is unfair."

- Ask what's the worst that could happen? Will you be boiled in hot lard? Will they take away your kids? Will you be tarred, feathered, and dragged down Main Street?

- Think of the situation you're facing as a video or board game; you have this puzzle to solve. What are the possibilities? What are your choices?

- Imagine how a strong leader whom you admire might handle this situation.

- Recall or even list times in the past when you overcame problems as bad as or worse than this one. What can you draw from those experiences? Can they at least help you keep this problem in perspective?

- Read stories of major obstacles or adversity that others have overcome in their lives. How does your problem compare? What can you learn from them?

- Force yourself to get moving by getting some exercise, taking a walk, or having a workout.

- Notice and label your thoughts as they pop into your head. "There's anger." "That's fear." "I feel sad." "There's a negative affirmation." Say them out loud either to yourself or a confidante. Write down or discuss alternatives.

- Think of your brain as another body organ, such as your stomach. Just as you might notice your empty stomach growling, you can notice "there goes my brain again being a worry wart." Or, "I see my brain is still clinging to that old hurt."

- Pretend your negative thoughts are loud, annoying commercials trying to sell you junk you don't need. You might respond with "Not today," "I am not buying that one," or, "Where is the mute button so I can silence your annoying drivel?"

- Schedule regular reflection time. Review your vision, values, and purpose. Read inspirational material. Meditate. Focus on life's bigger issues and put today's concerns into context.

Count your blessings, not your things.

CULTIVATE YOUR ATTITUDE OF GRATITUDE

"Why gaze down the sewers when there is loveliness all around us? One may find some fault in even the greatest masterpieces of art, music, and literature. But isn't it better to enjoy their charm and glory?"

Paramahansa Yogananda (1893–1952), an Indian yogi and guru

It's better to appreciate what I can't have than to have what I can't appreciate. One way to live in poverty is to have enough, but to focus on all that's missing and jealously look at what others have or have accomplished. Too often, we put off living. We're convinced that we'll be happier when we get promoted, pay off the mortgage, raise our kids, hit retirement, get that new car, renovate the house, lose those pounds, get away on vacation, find a better job, get married, get divorced... but tomorrow might never come. Live in the now.

A number of studies in the fields of happiness, positive psychology, and depression are showing profound and lasting benefits from teaching people the skills of counting their blessings, savoring things, appreciating beauty or quality, looking for the good in each day, and expressing gratitude.

Things I Think I Own

Today I stood at my window and
cursed the pouring rain.

Today a desperate farmer prayed for
his fields of grain.

My weekend plans are ruined; it
almost makes me cry,

While the farmer lifts his arms and
blesses the clouded sky.

The alarm went off on Monday and I
cursed my work routine.

Next door a laid-off worker feels the
empty pocket of his jeans.

I can't wait for my vacation, some
time to take for me.

He doesn't know, tonight, how he'll
feed his family.

I cursed my leaky roof and the grass
I need to mow.

A homeless man downtown checks
for change in the telephone.

I need a new car; mine is getting
really old.

He huddles in a doorway, seeking
shelter from the cold.

With blessings I'm surrounded: the
rain, a job, a home,

Though my eyes are often blinded by
the things I think I own.

Author Unknown

Gratitude Tips and Techniques

- On your own or with your spouse, wrap up your day just before going to bed by recounting at least three accomplishments or highlights of that day. This is especially important when you've had a bad day. Fall asleep feeling good about yourself and your situation. This can also be a great family exercise around the dinner table.

- Develop and keep expanding your Blessings and Brag list. List every accomplishment, strength, and success you've ever had or thing you're grateful for. Make it as long as possible and keep it growing. Review the list whenever you're feeling down on yourself, anxious, or a little sour.

- Take a "bliss break" by making a list of all the little things that you really enjoy. It's a fun exercise. Indulge yourself in activities on your list, which can run to many pages once you get started.

- Make a gratitude visit. Pick a person in your life whom you'd like to thank. Write this person a letter outlining how he or she helped you. After you've written it, call the person and ask to visit. Read the letter aloud when you are face-to-face.

- Study art, design, or natural wonders. Look with awe at the details, creativity, or beauty.

- Stop and treasure every accomplishment and success for yourself, loved ones, friends, and colleagues. Go out for dinner, take time off, send a personal note, raise a glass, give flowers, or buy the coffees.

TO KEEP YOU GROWING Here's where you can find more of my material on the topics covered in this chapter.

www.JimClemmer.com

- "When Choosing Our Thoughts We Choose Our Future" at http://www.jimclemmer.com/thoughts.
- "Seeing Only What Is or What Could Be" at http://www.jimclemmer.com/seeing.
- "Personal Visioning Pathways and Pitfalls" at http://www.jimclemmer.com/visioning.

Books

- Chapters Seven, "Picturing Your Preferred Future," and Nine, "Purpose," of *Pathways to Performance: A Guide to Transforming Yourself, Your Team, and Your Organization.*
- "Choosing Our Explanations and Our Happiness," "Changing Our Explanatory Style," and "Deepening Our Discipline and Commitment with Affirmations" along with dozens of Personal Application Ideas in *Growing the Distance: Self-Study System.*

XI

A balancing act high above the line.

RECLAIM YOUR TIME, RECLAIM YOUR LIFE

"I never could have done what I have done without the habits of punctuality, order, and diligence, without the determination to concentrate myself on one subject at a time..."

Charles Dickens (1812–1870), prolific English journalist who published over a dozen major novels, a large number of short stories, a handful of plays, and several nonfiction books

Leaders take control of their calendars and their lives. Leaders know that they don't have to be accessible to everyone all the time. Leaders strive for balance. Leaders know they don't have to answer every electronic message. Leaders look for leverage points and focus there. Leaders sort through the chaff of data and information to find the wheat of true communication. Leaders set priorities then reset them if conditions change. Leaders prune low-value tasks and maintain stop-doing lists. Leaders don't confuse busyness and quantity with quality. Leaders know that blaming technology for sucking time away is like blaming the car for speeding. So they have found ways to tame and leverage technology. Leaders realize that being frustrated by endless streams of poorly run meetings and not doing anything to influence change is feeding the Meeting Monster.

In the "no" so people don't "should" on you.

MANAGE YOUR OWN TIME OR SOMEONE ELSE WILL

"You can feel like a tin can surrounded by a circle of a hundred powerful magnets. Pulled at once in every direction, you go nowhere but instead spin faster and faster on your axis. In part, many people are excessively busy because they allow themselves to respond to every magnet: tracking too much data, processing too much information, answering to too many people, taking on too many tasks—all out of a sense that this is the way they must live in order to keep up and stay in control. But it's the magnets that have the control."[35]

Edward M. Hallowell, Crazy Busy: Overstretched, Overbooked, and About to Snap

If you're feeling overwhelmed and frantically busy, you're letting others "should" on you. That is you should always be available, your door should always be open, you should respond to every message, you should attend every meeting you're invited to, you should do whatever your boss asks, you should listen to every co-worker's "grump dump," you should have that expensive car, you should provide your kids with what they want, you should do it yourself to make sure it's done right, you should be perfect, you should multitask, you should take on that new project, you should sleep less, eat on the run, and skip exercise to get it all done ... you should do all that's asked of you. By everyone.

But ... should you?

We've had decades of time-management studies that come to the same conclusion: people who get the most done and maintain a balanced life invest their precious time like a tightwad looking to stretch every nickel to its maximum buying power. "Sorry" isn't the hardest word for most people; "no" is.

Effective leaders are focused and strategic with their time. In their article entitled "Beware the Busy Manager," professors Heike Bruch and Sumantra Ghoshal report: "After observing scores of managers for many years, we came to the conclusion that managers who take effective action (those who make difficult — even seemingly impossible — things happen) rely on a combination of two traits: focus and energy... aware of the value of time, they manage it carefully. Some refuse to respond to electronic messages, phone calls, or visitors outside certain periods of the day... they decide first what they must achieve and then work to manage the external environment...refusal to let other people or organizational constraints set the agenda — is perhaps the subtlest and most important distinction between this group of managers and all the rest."[136]

Tips and Techniques to Take Back Your Time

"Work while you work,
Play while you play;
One thing each time.
That is the way.

All that you do,
Do with your might;
Things done by halves
Are not done right."

McGuffey's Eclectic Primer, *William Holmes McGuffey (1800–1873) American professor and college president best known for writing the* McGuffey Readers, *120 million of which were sold between 1836 and 1960*

- Ensure that your day planner and calendar reflect your values. Schedule personal and professional activities that are aligned to your values. Don't allow today's pressures to crowd out what's really important in your life.

- Analyze your calendar and meeting agendas for the past few months. Do they clearly reflect your top goals and priorities?

- Get time-management training through the many books, courses, Internet resources, counseling, and other options that are widely available.

- Clean up and organize your electronic in-box(es), computer files and your office to minimize distractions and time wasted looking for data or materials.

- When reviewing your to-do list, first tackle the highest priority things that you most dread; get them out of the way and make the rest of your list easier.

- If lack of time is your reason for not investing more in your personal growth and development, figure out what's chewing up all of your time. For one month, keep a log of how you spend each fifteen minute block of your day from the time you get up until the time you go to bed. Before you start, develop categories such as reading, learning, meetings, family time, relaxation, travel, telephone calls, visiting, preparing, planning, etc. Estimate how much time you spend on each activity before you start your log. Once your log is complete, compare your estimates to the way you actually use your time. Then compare how you use your time to your vision, values, purpose, and strengths. You will find key areas for change and further growth.

- Do your most demanding creative mental work during your peak performance time. If you're a morning person, do it then. If you're a night owl, save it for that time. Find a quiet time or place and close your door or hang out a "Do Not Disturb" sign.

TAME YOUR E-BEAST

"I'm addicted to e-mail. My endorphins spike when I get a message. And when there are no messages, loneliness and despair overcome me."

Comic strip character Dilbert

One above-the-line leader I came across a few years ago was heading out on vacation. She did not want to return to an overflowing electronic in-box and have to spend days trying to catch up and read them all. So she put an auto responder on her electronic in-boxes. Every person who sent her a message received this response: "I am on vacation until the 15th. To be fully recharged and ready to jump back in when I return, I will not be checking my messages. When I get back to my office, I will delete all messages received while on vacation. So please call or visit me when I get back. If it's really important, resend your message then."

That strategy is extreme — too extreme for some. It's a powerful example, however, of controlling technical tools rather than letting those tools control you. Studies are showing electronic messages typically consume anywhere from 20 to 40 percent of most people's days. Many consider one-third to one-half of that time to be wasted and adding huge amounts of stress to their lives.

E-Beast Taming Tips and Techniques

- Turn off all pop-ups, texting, Instant Messages, and notifications of new messages when you're in a meeting or concentrating on a task. Check your messages at a few set times per day and stick to a strict time budget. Review them all quickly, then prioritize and start with the most critical.

- Train your co-workers, boss, and fellow team members not to expect instant electronic message responses from you. If the issue is urgent, suggest that they phone or visit you.

- Set clear boundaries around when you will not be available and won't be responding to electronic messages. You might use The 7:00–7:00 Rule; you're not responding to electronic messages between 7:00 PM and 7:00 AM on days off, holidays, or weekends. If you do want to take care of some messages during those hours, compose or reply but set them to send only during your work hours. That way, people won't get accustomed to you breaking your own Rule.

- Don't leave messages sitting in your in-box(es). File, delete, or reply to all of them within the time frame you've allocated.

- Turn off all communication devices when you're in meetings.

- Never send a message or text if you're feeling emotional, or the message could be misconstrued. Have a conversation.

- If you're part of an e-discussion that is circling back and forth, pick up the phone, arrange a meeting, or when possible, go to that person's office.

- Establish ground rules or protocols with your team, co-workers, and boss on how you use technology (such as in the next two points).

- Ensure your messages or texts have relevant subject lines, clear expectations of the receiver, and timelines right up front in the first screen the viewer sees.

- With such a high volume of messages and texts, most are not read, but rather scanned. Use bullet points, short sentences, and summaries. Include attachments, links, or more detail below those keys, if the reader needs it.

- Don't hide behind technology by sending messages that have emotional content which might hurt feelings or be misconstrued. Have those difficult or courageous conversations in person.

- Avoid short forms and acronyms unless you're very sure the recipients understand them.

- Use spell- and grammar-check programs and proper punctuation to convey an image of care and competence.

- Take training to strengthen your written communication skills and personal organization habits.

TO KEEP YOU GROWING — Here's where you can find more of my material on the topics covered in this chapter.

www.JimClemmer.com

- A selection of articles on Passion, Commitment, and Self-Discipline at http://www.jim clemmer.com/passion.
- Type "e-mail beast" (with the quotation marks) into the search engine on our site to read articles and a series of discussions and items on this topic in my **blog** and *The Leader Letter*.
- A selection of my writing and reader discussions on Passion, Commitment, and Self-Discipline from my **blog** and **monthly newsletter** at http://www.jimclemmer.com/newsletter/?cat=24.

Books

- Chapter Thirteen, "Establishing Goals and Priorities, Getting Organized, and Managing Time" of *Pathways to Performance: A Guide to Transforming Yourself, Your Team, and Your Organization*.
- "Deep Discipline" section in Chapter Five of *Growing the Distance: Timeless Principles for Personal, Career, and Family Success*.

XII

Grow ahead and make your day.

SLOW DOWN AND LIVE NOW

"There is more to life than increasing its speed."

Mohandas Karamchand Gandhi (1869–1948),
major political and spiritual leader of India and the
Indian independence movement

In my late forties, I bought myself a summer toy: a two-seat roadster convertible. At first, Heather was just indulging me when she agreed to go along on a few rides. Fairly quickly, though, she got into the joy of cruising along tree-lined country roads as we chatted, basked in the sunshine, and sang along to our favorite music.

On warm weather "cruising days," when I am heading out on business, instead of attempting the insanity that is the 401 highway, I have found a variety of quiet back-road alternatives. It does take extra time for these trips, but even so, I am struck by how often we choose the much faster expressway, where the top is up, the wind doesn't ruffle our hair (or my expanding forehead), and our "scenery" is roaring trucks and tailgaters who are closer than they appear.

Because it's the journey, not the destination, that's most

important in life. But we're so often so intent on getting to our next destination that we miss the joy of the trip. We're busy rushing toward our next goal. When we arrive, there's no time to savor it or look around before setting our sights on a new goal and off we rush again.

Mindfulness Tips and Techniques

- Pay attention to when time flies and you think, "When can I do this again?" and to when time drags and you think, "When will this ever be over?" What are you doing during those times? What does this tell you about ways to make your life more enjoyable?

- Practice regular meditation to keep yourself centered and relaxed. Take meditation training or experiment with this powerful force on your own. For a wealth of meditation resources, perspectives, tips, and approaches, do an Internet or book search on "meditation techniques."

- Study books that deal with deeper issues like the soul, mysticism, spirituality, prayer, purpose, and meaning. Combine this with meditation and reflection.

- Watch your mind. Monitor your thoughts. You might even say out loud, "There's worry," "I see anxiety is back," or, "Today's to-do list is clamoring for attention."

- Adopt the mind of a photographer. Be still. See the light, texture, and colors around you. Observe without judging.

- Imagine you're a novelist writing about the scene around you. Describe the setting and mood.

- Feel your own presence and inner energy field. Notice your breathing and the pressure on your buttocks or feet where you sit or stand.

- Get in the habit of monitoring your emotional state. "How am I feeling right now?" Observe your "monkey mind" (how Eastern philosophers describe our racing thoughts) and smile as you watch it racing to chase one shiny thought after another.

- Look for the lessons in negative events. What do you think you'll be saying you learned from this five or ten years from now? Is this event waking you up or slowing down your racing thoughts so you can be present in the Now?

MIND YOUR HERE AND NOW

"Happy the man, and happy he alone, He who can call today his own; He who secure within can say: Tomorrow do thy worst, for I have lived today."

Horace (65–8 BC), Roman lyric poet who exerted major influence on English poetry

Think of times you've felt high energy and most alive. They're typically when you're so engaged in what you're doing, the people you're with, the conversation you're having, the beauty you're experiencing, that you forget yourself and become totally engaged in what's happening right now. You lose track of time. At that point, you're not thinking about the problems of the past or worrying about the future. You're fully present in the Now.

Training on how to access that "happy place" within ourselves is very accessible today. Buddhist monks are the Olympic athletes of mindfulness. Jon Kabat-Zinn, founder of the pioneering Stress Reduction Clinic at the University of Massachusetts Medical Center observes, "Buddhist meditation is leading to an expansion of the science of what it means to be human."[137]

In *The Power of Now*, Eckhart Tolle writes, "Life is now. There was never a time when your life was *not* now, nor will there ever be…the present moment is all you ever have. There is never a time when your life is not 'this moment'…you cannot be both unhappy *and* fully present in the Now… problems are mind-made and need time to survive…they cannot survive in the actuality of the Now."[138]

TAKE CARE OF YOUR MIND, BODY, AND SPIRIT

A road sign on a winding mountain highway warned, "Slow Down or Die." Simple, succinct, and great life advice as well. If day after day of stressful racing around doesn't manage to physically kill us before our time, it will surely kill our happiness and enjoyment in being here.

Self-Care Tips and Techniques

- Physical fitness is a big factor in how we feel. If you need to get into shape, consider a personal trainer, nutritional counseling, a weight-loss program based on lifestyle change (not fad diets), a "fitness buddy," or join a gym or recreational club.
- Be sure you take vacations and regular time off to recharge your batteries and keep your life in balance.
- Reward yourself for reaching milestones along the way. Build a sense of progress and momentum.
- Get involved in fundraising or volunteer with charitable organizations or social service agencies.
- Spend time with "meaning seekers" who are engaged in finding a deeper spirit and meaning in their lives.
- Participate in spiritual workshops or personal retreats providing guidance for your inner quest.
- Don't confuse religion and spirituality. Religion prescribes a particular system of faith and worship, usually based on rigid dogmas and right/wrong ways of living. Spirituality is the quest for

deeper meaning and understanding of our divine nature in universal laws. Spirituality can be approached in many ways and take numerous forms of expression. Someone who goes hiking and thinks about God is more spiritually focused than someone else who goes to church and thinks about hiking.

Live Below Your Means

"He who is not thrifty is a slave to circumstance. Fate says, 'Do this or starve,' and if you have no surplus saved up you are the plaything of chance, the pawn of circumstance, the slave of some one's caprice, a leaf in a storm."[139]

Elbert Hubbard (1856–1915), American writer, publisher, artist, and philosopher

The more savings you have, the less you're beholden to an annoying boss, the economy, or sudden job loss. Early in my career, I started a "drop dead" savings fund. This money was to allow me or Heather to tell any bad boss to get lost, and survive a job loss, or start our own business. It's been the fallback factor enabling us to do what we do because we want to — not because we have to. Without this financial cushion, the chances of being exploited by a bad boss or getting stuck in a soul-destroying job are much higher. Debt can be a ruthless master.

As your income rises, don't raise your standard of living. Keep it constant or even lower. Put all of your additional money into savings. Pay yourself first and have savings automatically deducted from your bank account on pay days, before you have a chance to spend it. Set a target of saving at least 10 percent of your income — shoot for 20 percent or more. Avoid borrowing money and pay off your mortgage as soon as you can. If you can't save up and pay cash for everything else, do you really need it or do you just want it? Wants, you can do without. Collect interest; don't pay it.

LET GO:
FORGIVE AND LIVE

"The sword of attack is always held backwards.
We think we're holding the handle, swinging our
blade at the world. In truth, though, we're gripping
the blade and waving about a harmless handle.
The harder we fight, the deeper we cut ourselves."[140]

Dan Cavicchio, Gardens from the Sand: A Story About
Looking for Answers and Finding Miracles

The dark energy of anger and resentment keeps us stuck in the past and blocks our enjoyment of the here and now. It's like burning down our homes to get rid of the mice. It's like carrying a sack around your neck with a sizeable stone being added for every single person you resent, every slight you hang on to, or every misdeed you remember. Forgive. Letting go of bitterness, hatred, and vengefulness is one of best things we can do for ourselves. It empties the sack of stones that's serving only to sink us deeper in that noxious swamp.

Forgiveness Tips and Techniques

- Don't saw sawdust. How much time do you spend looking back with regret, guilt, or bitterness? We can only draw lessons from the past and move on; we cannot change it. We can only change what lies ahead.

- Do you need to forgive people in order to drop that heavy load? As much as you might feel they don't deserve it, forgive them for your sake. Rid yourself of the toxins and move on.

- Resolve conflicts with others early, before they escalate and grow out of hand. Be the first to say, "I am sorry," and reconcile the disagreement.

TO KEEP YOU GROWING *Here's where you can find more of my material on the topics covered in this chapter.*

www.JimClemmer.com

- A selection of articles on Deepening Spirit, Meaning, and Purpose at http://www.jimclemmer.com/meaning.
- A selection of articles on Attitude and Outlook at http://www.jimclemmer.com/attitude.
- Type "wind in our hair" (with the quotation marks) into the search engine on our site to read a series of discussions and items on slowing down and living now in my **blog** and **monthly newsletter**.
- A selection of my writing and reader discussions on Deepening Spirit, Meaning, and Purpose from my **blog** and **monthly newsletter** at http://www.jimclemmer.com/newsletter/?cat=25.

Books

- "Checking My Spirit" and "Spirit and Meaning: Personal Application Ideas" in *Growing the Distance: Self-Study System*.
- "Choosing to Let Go of Deadly Emotions" in *Growing the Distance: Timeless Principles for Personal, Career, and Family Success*.

XIII

What you don't grow can hurt you.

GROW YOUR COURAGE

"Twenty years from now you will be more disappointed by the things that you didn't do than the ones you did do. So throw off the bowlines. Sail away from the safe harbor. Catch the trade winds in your sails. Explore. Dream. Discover."

Samuel Langhorne Clemens (1835–1910), known as "Mark Twain," American author and humorist

The evening before a speaking engagement in Vancouver, I was in a hotel room on the 37th floor overlooking Stanley Park, English Bay, and The Lion's Gate Bridge. After a pleasant dinner with a friend, I returned to my room. The sun was setting on a beautiful, warm spring evening. Wanting to enjoy the view, I took my cell phone out onto the balcony to check my voice mail. When I turned to go back in my room, I found that the sliding door to the balcony was locked. The latch had fallen into place as I closed it behind me.

I called the hotel on my cell phone and a manager was sent to help. He, however, could not get into my room, either. It seems the night latch had swung into place behind me when I entered the room. So he went into the room next door, came out on its balcony, adjoined to mine, and stepped over the small railing separating us so he could help me get back into my room and undo the night latch from the inside.

We tried lifting the door out of the frame or unlatching it. It would not budge. Ten minutes later, a maintenance man arrived bearing a three-foot-long flat steel rod. He unscrewed the frame from the sliding door, slid the steel through, and unlatched it.

It's so easy to lock doors behind ourselves and not realize what's happened until it's too late. Whether we just accept our fate or find ways or help to unlock those doors depends upon whether we've been living mostly above or below the line.

Words of Advice: Courageous Leadership Experience

Discussions of courageous leadership at home and at work created one of the largest responses I've ever had in my blog and newsletter. Here's good advice that emerged from Bryan Mayhann, in Boston, MA:

- "Gathering information when making decisions can increase your courage to act ('act on fact'). However, too much analysis can leave you second-guessing your gut, and paralyze you.

- "Embrace and stay connected to something larger than you. Courage to act is often more likely when you are founded upon a rock that is larger than yourself (such as core beliefs, religion, community, family, or other entity). By having that source of order and strength to draw from during your 'trial,' you can be confident and courageous that even if you fail, you are still sustained by something beyond yourself. Yes, leading is lonely. But sometimes we make it much lonelier than it has to be.

- "Don't let past poor judgment paralyze you. It is easy to feel that since you failed once (or twice, etc.,)... that you are now a failure. If you subscribe to that, you'll let that self-doubt paralyze you. Instead, realize that because you have failed... you are now smarter. You now have more experience than before, and so are more qualified to make the next decision... rather than less."

Karen Eisler from Regina, Saskatchewan, shared these practical how-to suggestions for building our courage:

- "Having enough courage to take the first step or first fall is the hardest part. The first part of that is self talk — if we talk to ourselves negatively then we already are in trouble. I will try to start something by thinking of the positive ending I want to see and working step by step toward it. I am surprised at some of the different decisions I make by thinking that way.

- "For example, with my teenage children, I start with what do I want them to learn from this situation in the end and I work from there. Or when I take a class; what do I want for an outcome of the class? It may be an A or it may be to keep my sanity and not sacrifice myself, my family or friends, and be OK with a lesser mark.

- "In work situations if I am afraid of doing something — for example talking to an employee about his or her attitude — I have found that the first step is the hardest. It's easier sometimes to ignore, walk away, or excuse away their behavior. But to start the conversation is the hardest part and that takes courage.

- "Part of courage is that it is OK to make a mistake and learn from it. Sometimes we are held back by our fear of making a mistake. If a child learning to walk is held back because of fear of failing (or falling) than s/he would never learn to walk. It is the repeated failure that helps him/her learn to walk."

COURAGEOUS PERSONAL CONVERSATIONS

"The easiest kind of relationship for me is with ten thousand people. The hardest is with one."

Joan Baez (1941–), Mexican-American folk
singer and songwriter

I was speaking to a group going through huge organizational changes as their industry experienced dramatic restructuring. We broke the auditorium into three sections with small discussion groups in each identifying what we're feeling, saying, and doing when dealing with these changes in leading, following, or wallowing mode. During the recap of each group's findings, we agreed that often we need to dip down below the line to vent briefly or let go of painful emotions during times of big changes in our personal or professional lives. I added that we may take therapeutic visits to Pity City, but it's a deadly place to live. A woman in the front row blurted out, "My husband is the mayor!"

I hope she was talking with him about that and constructively challenging or reframing his thinking. Less effective relationships — many of which don't last — are characterized by poor quality and quantity of communications. Often that's because of low courage, skill, or under-appreciating just how critical those courageous conversations really are.

Psychologist and author of *The 100 Simple Secrets of Relationships* David Niven reports,

"Couples who never argue are 35 percent more likely to divorce. On the surface, that seems like a strange finding, since we associate arguments with bad outcomes, but an inability to share frustration is a dangerous thing. If you don't argue, [frustrations] build up within you until they get bigger and bigger."[141] Of course, the quality of those arguments — staying on message about the problems, issue, or specific behavior and not making personal attacks or put-downs — is also critical.

Courage-Building Tips and Techniques

- Contribute to authentic conversations in an authentic workplace. Speak the truth as you see it. Obviously the time and place need to be appropriate. Diplomacy and tact are also critical. Help others (especially your peers and those above you) to see the moose-on-the-table.

- Address any conflicts or moose-on-the-table issues if they are getting in the way of your job satisfaction. If you can't resolve them, it may be time to move on. Don't be a victim.

- If your work needs realignment, talk with your boss about your values, strengths and what you'd like to change in order to be more effective.

- Do you feel that you have a reasonable level of choice and freedom to express yourself at work? If not, what are you doing to ensure you don't further become a victim?

- If you have tried your hardest to change your team or organization and can't, it may be time for you to find other opportunities. Life is too short to be a victim of a toxic workplace.

- Remind your team that cowardly potshots, put-downs, or sniping comments aren't acceptable behavior inside or outside meetings. Above-the-line humor or good-natured teasing can add positive energy to your laughter index, and that's important. A simple and effective technique to stop below-the-line zingers is to have team members tap on a glass or the table with a pen when they hear a negative crack.

PUT UP OR SHUT UP

*"But the bravest are surely those who have the clearest
vision of what is before them, glory and danger alike,
and yet notwithstanding go out and meet it."*

Thucydides (460–395 BC), *Greek historian and author
of the* History of the Peloponnesian War

It doesn't take much courage to join in with the hecklers at the back of Bitter Bus in Pity City. It is infinitely easier to lean back and take potshots at people living and leading above the line than to get there yourself. Clever sarcasm and scathing wit can be entertaining. Some comedians make a good living poking fun at all that's wrong.

In an organization or team, though, wrapping a serious message or feedback in a "humorous zinger" is gutless. When the object of the derision takes offense, the cowardly corporate comedian can respond with a lame, "Hey, I was only kidding. Can't you take a joke?" It takes true courage to live and lead above the line, especially when the rest of your team or organization is wallowing in the cynicism swamp. Some studies have shown it takes up to five times more energy and effort to be optimistic in the face of a group's overwhelming pessimism. Building courageous leadership that increases positive energy is what leads to happiness, better health, higher team morale, and peak organizational performance.

So either put up or shut up. Stop with the mean-spirited jokes or even rolls of your eyes. You're either adding to your team or organization's cowardice or its courage. If you're not yet far enough along on your courage scale to counteract the pessimism around you, at least don't add to the negative energy by wallowing around in the muck with the cynics, cowards, and wannabe stand-ups.

Pretty soon, you'll find they aren't all that funny.

TO KEEP YOU GROWING

Here's where you can find more of my material on the topics covered in this chapter.

www.JimClemmer.com

- A selection of articles on Fostering Openness and Transparency at http://www.jim clemmer.com/openness.
- Type "courage" or "courageous leadership" or "courageous conversations" (with the quotation marks) into the search engine on our site to read articles and a series of discussions and items in my **blog** and **monthly newsletter**.
- A selection of my writing and reader discussions on Fostering Openness and Transparency from my **blog** and **monthly newsletter** at http://www.jimclemmer.com/ newsletter/?cat=6.

Books

- For supervisors, managers, and executives – Chapter Three, "Responsibility for Choices and "The Moose on the Table" section in Chapter Four of *The Leader's Digest: Timeless Principles for Team and Organization Success*.
- Management team assessments, application ideas, and planning exercises in the "Responsibility for Choices" and "Authenticity" sections of *The Leader's Digest: Practical Application Planner*.
- A central theme in *Moose on the Table®* is fictional character Pete Leonard's battle with cowardice and courage. Go to www.mooseonthetable.com for video clips explaining each chapter and an overview of the book.

XIV

Weak boss? You can wallow, follow, or lead.

UPWARD LEADERSHIP: LEADING YOUR BOSS

"Leading up requires great courage and determination....but we all carry a responsibility to do what we can when it will make a difference. Upward leadership is not a natural skill, but it can be mastered."[142]

Michael Useem, *Leading Up: How to Lead Your Boss So You Both Win*

If you're working for an ineffective or substandard boss, you have plenty of company. Of the 1,118 people who completed a survey at the Badbossology.com web site "48 percent said they would fire their boss if they could, 29 percent would have their boss assessed by a workplace psychologist and 23 percent would send their boss for management training." Cofounder Ian Donen says, "These results seem consistent with psychologist Dr. Robert Hogan's suggestion that at least 55 percent of managers in America are incompetent."[143]

No doubt those who would visit a bad boss web site are feeling more than a little disgruntled with their manager! But negative feelings about bosses abound. A careerbuilder.com survey showed "nearly 30 percent of workers said they were unhappy with their supervisors."[144] Many people lose the boss lottery and, through no fault of their own, end up reporting to an ineffective manager.

In dealing with a bad boss, we have four choices: 1. Wallow as a victim while complaining and increasing our stress. 2. Live with him or her because other parts of your work compensate for the irritation. 3. Fire your boss by moving out of that job to find another boss (or become your own). 4. Practice upward leadership.

The Crow and the Pitcher

A Crow, half-dead with thirst, came upon a Pitcher which had once been full of water, but when the Crow put its beak into the mouth of the Pitcher he found that only very little water was left and that he could not reach far enough down to get at it. He tried, and he tried, but at last had to give up in despair. Then a thought came to him, and he took a pebble and dropped it into the Pitcher. Then he took another pebble and dropped it into the Pitcher. And another, and another, until at last, after casting in a few more pebbles, he saw the water mount up near him. Thus he was able to quench his thirst and save his life.

Little by little does the trick.
Aesop's Fables

UNDERSTAND WHY YOUR BOSS IS BAD

"If you think your boss is stupid, remember: you wouldn't have a job if he was any smarter."

John Gotti (1940–2002), American organized-crime boss

Some bad bosses are bad people. Their personal relationships are disasters, they're miserably unhappy, and their values come from the dark side like vapors wafting from the swamp. They live to dominate and bully the people under them.

But that's not the case with most: most bad bosses aren't bad people. They are good people doing a bad job. Many are blithely unaware of the dead, wounded, or stressed-out bodies they leave in their wake. Just as most of us rate ourselves as above average drivers (no one's sure who's having all the accidents), bad bosses tend to think they're good examples of strong leadership. Understanding how your well-intentioned

boss has gone off the rails can help you choose the best strategy for managing him or her. Here are common reasons good people can become bad bosses:

Confusing information with communication: When many managers want increased communication, they fire off more messages or beef up intranet sites. They don't realize their overuse of technology is causing information overload and creating a barrier to conversation and human connections. They mistakenly think they're reaching out.

Micromanagement: Bad bosses are often micromanagers poking into every detail of every decision and facet of the business. This may be because their own bosses expect them to know or be answerable for every little detail. This often leads to the boss believing that having people put in face time or looking really busy is more important than whether the desired results were achieved. It's also possible that bosses micromanage because they were burned or embarrassed by someone else's past poor performance and they want to make sure that never happens again.

It's all they know: Many bad bosses have had no role model other than another ineffective boss. Maybe they watched an executive yell his or her way to the top. Maybe they saw micromanagement result in promotions. Or maybe they're now working for a bad boss and mimicking that behavior; often bad bosses promote in their own image. So you now work for a clone of that ineffectiveness, a level or two above your boss.

Promoted for all the wrong reasons: Organizations pay a lot of lip service to the importance of leadership, staff, and other warmed-over motherhood statements. But only the very best organizations actually measure and use leadership skills as a key promotion criterion. In most cases, people are promoted for qualities such as strong technical or analytical skills, loyalty, or likeability because they are good political players and butt kissers. And some people are of course promoted for strong short-term results, despite the damaged morale and walking wounded they've created.

Overworked and undertrained: Many managers aren't coping well with today's relentless pressure to do more with less. They feel they need to push harder to get more from everyone in their organization. They have bosses pushing them. At the same time, too few have been given training on management methods — such as effectively mapping and managing processes based on solid data — to work smarter, not harder. Most have not had good training and coaching in people-leadership skills to effectively lead teams and coach. Many bosses reflect their organization's mindset that training is a nice-to-do when there's time, or even a sign of weakness.

Feeble feedback: Many bad bosses don't know what they don't know because nobody tells them. At the same time, they don't really want to know what the people they lead think about how they could be more effective. Bad bosses often rate their own leadership performance very highly. Tragically, they choke off communication channels and misread the lack of feedback as a sign they are doing well, because no one is telling them otherwise. And they like it just fine that way.

Boss Leadership Tips and Techniques

"Everyday leaders are quiet catalysts who push back against prevailing norms, create learning, and lay the groundwork for slow but ongoing organizational and social change... by acting as agents of 'positive deviation' by instigating small wins and creating learning, by pushing people and systems to confront their latent conflicts and adaptive challenges, by organizing other people to act together toward shared goals, and by inspiring change and people."[145]

> Debra E. Meyerson, Tempered Radicals: How People Use Difference to Inspire Change at Work

- Do you know what keeps those above you in the organization awake at night? What their key goals and priorities are? Don't wait to be told — find out.

- Learn to leverage your organization's relationship dynamics. This involves strengthening trust, persuasion, and influence skills. Build networks and coalitions, especially if you're trying to influence significant change.

- If you're feeling overwhelmed, draw up a list of what you're working on, with time frames or the estimated effort and resources required, and set the priorities as you see them. Regularly review and adjust this list with your boss. Be especially sure to get agreement on priority order. When your boss comes to you with urgent new priorities, pull out your list and discuss where those fit in and what should be moved down or off your list.

- Don't ever badmouth or put down your boss to co-workers. If you need to get input from others on dealing with your boss, focus on the behavior, issues, or problems, not the person.

- Ensure your boss gets credit for successes. Look for opportunities to recognize or reinforce his or her strengths and the kind of leadership behavior you'd like to see more of. Make a list of your boss's greatest strengths and biggest weaknesses and see if there are ways you can build upon the strengths and reduce the weaknesses.

- Pick your timing and approach. You may need to wait for the right opportunity to approach your boss. Is he or she more receptive at particular times of the day, in meetings or one-on-one, by conversation or with a carefully crafted proposal? Are you approaching your boss in your own preferred style or your boss's? If your boss is analytical, do you lead with facts and analysis? If he or she is results-focused, do you focus first on results? If your boss is strong on relationships and people connections, do you focus on the human touch?

- What could you learn by watching others who have a stronger relationship with your boss?

- Use technology effectively. If your boss mainly communicates through electronic channels, respond in kind for most routine matters. However, if he or she sends you a critical electronic message or gets into sensitive personal issues, never respond in kind. Phone or pay a visit to avoid misunderstandings and escalating emotions. You may need to follow up a phone conversation with an electronic message documenting what you discussed.

- Strengthen your credibility. Make sure you are acting as you say, demonstrating the leadership behavior you'd like to see from your boss. The single biggest source of your personal credibility with your boss is meeting your commitments. Make sure you do what you say you're going to do, and never overpromise or underdeliver.

- Don't be a victim. If you work for a truly awful boss, leading him or her is likely impossible. Your best strategy may be to minimize contact, build support networks within your organization, develop strong relationships with your boss's peers or managers, or get out of that reporting relationship.

www.JimClemmer.com

- A selection of articles on Serving, Influencing and Leading Upward at http://www.jim clemmer.com/serving.
- Type "upward leadership" (with the quotation marks) into the search engine on our web site for articles and a series of discussions and items in my **blog** and **monthly newsletter**.
- A selection of my writing and reader discussions on Serving, Influencing, and Leading Upward from my **blog** and **monthly newsletter** at http://www.jimclemmer.com/ newsletter/?cat=4.

Books

- In *Moose on the Table®* a major storyline is fictional character Pete Leonard's struggle with his bully boss, Doug Drake (the name means "dark river" and "dragon"). Go to www.mooseonthetable.com for video clips explaining each chapter and an overview of the book.
- See sections "I'm in Charge," "Leading from the middle," and "Making the best of a bad boss," in Chapter Three of *The Leader's Digest: Timeless Principles for Team and Organization Success.*
- Management team assessments, application ideas, and planning exercises in the "Responsibility for Choices" sections of *The Leader's Digest: Practical Application Planner.*

XV

*Our Interconnections and Influence
help us thrive beyond our I-land*

GET HELP, GET CONNECTED, AND GET PERSUASIVE

"In a real sense all life is inter-related. All persons are caught in an inescapable network of mutuality, tied in a single garment of destiny. Whatever affects one directly affects all indirectly. I can never be what I ought to be until you are what you ought to be, and you can never be what you ought to be until I am what I ought to be. This is the inter-related structure of reality."

Martin Luther King, Jr. (1929–1968),
American clergyman, activist, and prominent leader
in the African-American civil rights movement

Our interconnectedness or oneness with each other and universal spirit has been taught for thousands of years in many spiritual, mystical, and native belief systems. The 17th century English metaphysical poet John Donne's line "no man is an island, entire of itself..." has become a truism. The 20th century Trappist monk and spiritual writer Thomas Merton wrote a book, Joan Baez performed a song, and a 1962 movie based on WWII hero George Ray Tweed were all titled "No Man is an Island."

The Internet is a powerful manifestation of our connectedness. In an incredibly short time, it has dramatically altered, interconnected, and affected our economies, social networks, healthcare, entertainment, learning definitions and methods, scientific understanding ... Globalized trade, international finance, immigration, and environmental issues like global warming also starkly illustrate what an interdependent and global village we've truly become.

Modern research on social intelligence — a key component of emotional intelligence — is further showing the effects of our interconnections. In *Social Intelligence: The New Science of Human Relationships*, Emotional Intelligence guru Daniel Goleman explores how "our reaction to others, and theirs to us, have a far-reaching biological impact, sending out cascades of hormone that regulate everything from our hearts to our immune systems, making good relationships act like vitamins — and bad relationships like poisons. We can 'catch' other people's emotions the way we catch a cold."[146]

And it's so easy now to "catch" emotions, 24 hours a day, wherever they are, in our tightly interconnected world.

Positive Connections: Tips and Techniques

"Keep away from people who try to belittle your ambitions. Small people always do that, but the really great make you feel that you, too, can become great."

> *Samuel Langhorne Clemens (1835–1910), known as "Mark Twain," American author and humorist*

- Unless you're trying to influence them, spend as little time as possible with the pessimists stuck in Pity City. Spend your time with optimistic leaders who live above the line.

- Develop or join a network of colleagues interested in personal growth. This can be a powerful source of learning from others' experiences. It's also a great way for you to reflect on your own experiences and articulate your improvement plans.

- A group that meets regularly is an excellent forum for making public declarations or even "contracts" of your personal improvement plans. This approach makes it much harder to back away from forming the tough new habits you know you need to develop.

ASK FOR HELP

"The strong individual is the one who asks
for help when he needs it. Whether he has
an abscess on his knee or in his soul."

Rona Barrett (1936–), American
columnist and entrepreneur

When faced with bad news, setbacks, or significant loss, a dangerous response is withdrawal. This can start the spiral of wallowing in our own negative thoughts and worries. The more we wallow, the further below the line we sink. The lower we slip, the more we wallow.

Most people quickly seek a doctor's help in mending a broken bone or treating a disease. Yet many people believe that asking for help with personal issues is a sign of weakness. Many believe they need to "suck it up" and get themselves out of the problem. But wallowing in our issues on our own is the easy way out — in the short term. It takes real courage to face our situations. It takes courage to acknowledge our interdependence and ask for help. It takes courage to be honest with someone about our struggles.

Support-Building Tips and Techniques

- For help with addictions, reach out to groups like Alcoholics Anonymous, Al-Anon (for relatives or friends of people with alcohol problems), or other trained professionals.

- If you, or someone you care for, suffer from depression, phobias, panic, debilitating stress/anxiety, eating or personality disorders, relationship difficulties, or other challenges, find a psychologist or psychotherapist trained in Cognitive Behavior Therapy.

- Find a coach, therapist, or counselor to guide you using the emerging new principles of strengths-based positive psychology.

- Identify a complementary partner in your business, on your team, or in your personal life, whose strengths are your weaknesses. Work together to balance each other. This won't always be easy or conflict-free. Practice give-and-take based on connections around your shared vision, values, and purpose.

- Do you need to increase your friendships and grow your social circle? Happiness and luck research shows that an active social life is a great positive.

- Be careful of withdrawing through choosing to watch television rather than reading a book. Psychological studies show that the average mood while watching TV sitcoms is mild depression. TV is the mindless way out and doesn't provide ongoing gratification. Don't just choose the 'easy pleasures.'

- Join sports, hobby, craft, or social groups or take classes to pursue your personal interests and stayed connected.

- If you're not part of a spiritual community, explore outlets that can help you develop or strengthen your beliefs and build your spiritual and social connections.

Wise Words on the Power of Persuasion

"Persuasion is a process, not an event. Rarely, if ever, is it possible to arrive at a shared solution on the first try. More often than not, persuasion involves listening to people, testing a position, developing a new position that reflects input from the group, more testing, incorporating compromises, and then trying again. If this sounds like a slow and difficult process, that's because it is. But the results are worth the effort."[147]

Jay Conger, "The Necessary Art of Persuasion"

"It is not sufficient to know what one ought to say, but one must know how to say it."

Aristotle (384 BC–322 BC), Rhetoric, Greek philosopher, a student of Plato, and teacher of Alexander the Great

"No matter how intellectually brilliant we may be, that brilliance will fail to shine if we are not persuasive. That is particularly true in fields where entry has high hurdles for cognitive abilities, like engineering and science, medicine and law, and executive ranks in general."[148]

Daniel Goleman, Working with Emotional Intelligence

STRENGTHEN YOUR INFLUENCE AND PERSUASION

"We often refuse to accept an idea merely because the tone of voice in which it has been expressed is unsympathetic to us."

Friedrich Wilhelm Nietzsche (1844–1900), German philosopher

A key element of leading others is to influence their thinking and behaviors. Our ability to influence depends on factors such as the strength of our relationship, our credibility, and trust levels with those we're trying to influence. It also involves how well we've covered the bases with other key influencers around the person or group we are trying to influence. And — as the emotional intelligence research shows (page 117) — our ability to influence calls for strong persuasion skills.

We've all found ourselves resisting someone else not because of what they are saying, but how they are saying it. They may strike us as arrogant, unfeeling, rude, or overly critical. Most of the friction in our relationships comes from the wrong tone of voice.

Less effective bosses or managers use position power and get people to do things because they have to. Leaders get people to do the same things because people want to. It's the same goal, but with a world of difference in execution and long-term results.

Expanding Your Web of Influence: Tips and Techniques

"First and foremost, the tempered radicals I have researched build supportive affiliations with people inside and outside their organizations… actions designed to create connections with others with similar values, beliefs, and identities, will further the impact of your efforts and help affirm your sense of self. Activities will be most effective if they have the potential to accumulate or to ripple into additional changes. They need not be immediately obvious as change-inducing."[149]

Debra E. Meyerson, Tempered Radicals: How People Use Difference to Inspire Change at Work

• Focus most of your energy on things within your control. Carefully pick areas or changes you would like to influence. Figure out how to let go of those things or circumstances over which you have no control. Don't "awfulize" them. Doing that just increases everyone's misery, especially your own.

• Go out of your way to take breaks or have lunch with people in your organization or team with whom you don't normally spend time. Get to know more people informally.

• Learn how your organizational game is played. Any organization of five people or more is political. Politics involve relationships, trust, power, persuasion, and influence.

• Build networks and coalitions, especially if you're trying to influence significant change. Work with those people who are ready to move forward and build momentum with you. Don't fixate on the fence-sitters, naysayers, or resisters. Involve your boss where appropriate.

www.JimClemmer.com

- A selection of articles on Communicating, Motivating, and Influencing at http://www.jimclemmer.com/motivating.
- A selection of my writing and reader discussions on Communicating, Motivating, and Influencing from my **blog** and **monthly newsletter** at http://www.jimclemmer.com/newsletter/?cat=26.

Books

- "Words Worth" in Chapter Eight of *Growing the Distance: Timeless Principles for Personal, Career, and Family Success.*
- "Increasing my Influence," "Inspiring through Verbal Communications," and "Personal Application Ideas" from the Mobilizing and Energizing section in *Growing the Distance: Self-Study System.*
- "Inspiring, Energizing, and Arousing" in Chapter Three and Personal "Pathways and Pitfalls" for communications in Chapter Twenty-One of *Pathways to Performance: A Guide to Transforming Yourself, Your Team, and Your Organization.*
- For supervisors, managers, and executives — "Speaking of Success" and "Powers of persuasion" in Chapter Eight of *The Leader's Digest: Timeless Principles for Team and Organization Success.*

XVI

*Your life is like a garden: you can let it go to
weed or you can get growing and lead.*

GROW FOR IT

*"Man's mind may be likened to
a garden, which may be intelligently
cultivated or allowed to run wild;
but whether cultivated or neglected,
it must, and will, bring forth. If no
useful seeds are put into it, then an
abundance of useless weed-seeds
will fall therein, and will continue
to produce their kind."*[150]

James Allen (1864–1912), As a Man Thinketh,
British writer of inspirational self-help books and poetry

A major theme underlying my books, workshops, our training and consulting services, and this book is that personal and leadership growth is critical to dealing with turbulence and change. Our personal and organizational lives are ever changing — often when we least expect it. Step one is accepting the change, rather than wallowing and complaining. Change simply is what it is. Step two is flexing ourselves or the change to fuel our personal, team, or organizational growth. Life is constant, endless, and unpredictable change. Change is inevitable. Growth or misery is optional.

The core themes from which the title grew for my fourth book, *Growing the Distance: Timeless Principles for Personal, Career, and Family Success,* are:

- Change or be changed. There are also two kinds of people: those who are changing and those who are setting themselves up to be victims of change.
- Change can't be managed. If the rate of external change exceeds our rate of internal growth, we're eventually going to be changed.
- Learning and continuous development are at the heart of an organization's or individual's ability to adapt to a rapidly changing environment.
- Leadership is a journey of personal discovery and learning. Learning needs to move from a phase of life to a way of life.
- We can't predict or manage change. Leaders and organizations that are built to last master change by embracing continuous growth, learning, and development.

Louis L'Amour (1908–1988), American author of 86 novels, 14 short-story collections, and one full-length work of nonfiction summarized it well: "The best of all things is to learn. Money can be lost or stolen, health and strength may fail, but what you have committed to your mind is yours forever."

On the Grow: Tips and Techniques

- Find a personal coach or counselor to guide your personal development. He or she can be a sounding board, gather feedback from those you work with, prod you to reach your goals, provide advice, and encourage you.

- Reflect and plan, every day. Read or listen to spiritual, inspiring, or educational material; write in your journal; daydream; review the previous day; set your priorities for the next day to sort out the urgent from the truly important; pray or meditate; and continue developing your vision, values, and purpose.

- Check out many of the excellent books available to inspire, instruct, and guide your personal, team, and organization improvement efforts. Many effective leaders are devoted readers.

- Try your hand at writing articles for your trade or association publications, local newspaper, or internal newsletter (many of these publications welcome such contributions). You could prepare a paper to deliver at a conference. Or write internal articles, training steps, and the like to share your experience and provide reflective learning.

- My early career time working with Dale Carnegie Training clearly showed me just how powerful developing public-speaking or verbal communication skills can be in building self-confidence and leadership skills. You don't have to be on your feet speaking to a group though that's a very effective way to stretch and grow. You can reflect on your experiences and talk about your improvement plans with team members, your manager, a personal coach or therapist, a close friend, or your spouse.

- Develop the habit of continually stretching outside your comfort zone a bit at a time. Daily or even just weekly stretches, however small, accumulate into powerful new habits and ever-stronger discipline muscles.

- Try to cultivate a mentor relationship with a senior manager or another seasoned person who would enjoy taking you under his or her wing. This could be an experienced HR or training professional or someone in a key technical or staff-support role. It could be anyone from whom you think you could learn.

"I am convinced that it is of primordial importance to learn more every year than the year before. After all, what is education but a process by which a person begins to learn how to learn."

Peter Ustinov (1921–2004), British actor, writer and dramatist

Rick Fullerton has been a Client, associate, fellow learner, and teacher. He's had extensive experience in both private and public sectors and been an adjunct professor in a faculty of management. He has designed and taught graduate-level courses on consulting, process facilitation, leadership, and organizational development. In a discussion with a number of my blog and newsletter readers, he provided solid advice on strategies for successful personal growth:

1. "Be clear about where you want to be, within a 3–5 year time frame. Be as specific as possible about the position or role you see for yourself. Validate this through conversations with mentors, current or potential managers, human resource professionals, and others to ensure that your goals are grounded in reality and represent an informed choice rather than a pipe dream.

2. "Get a crisp, clear picture of where you are today using tools such as multi-source feedback, self-assessment instruments, formal appraisals, and updated resumes. Use these inputs to produce an inventory of strengths and developmental challenges.

3. "Focus on those critical few skills that will allow noticeable progress. Select two strengths to sustain and two challenges to develop. It is vitally important to maintain focus on strengths while addressing one or two areas that require attention, since changing less effective behaviors can be difficult. People often report improvement in both strengths and challenges.

4. "Create personal improvement plans, identify measures for tracking progress, set specific targets to be achieved, and design feedback loops. You can employ a wide range of tracking tools, such as learning journals, action logs, mini-360 surveys, physical measures (e.g. weight, heart rate), job observations (watch me, give me feedback) and more."

HOW I KEEP MYSELF CURRENT

"We must always change, renew, rejuvenate ourselves; otherwise we harden."

Johann Wolfgang von Goethe (1749–1832), one of Germany's most influential writers of poetry, drama, literature, theology, philosophy, humanism, and science

A *Leader Letter* reader asked me how I keep my skills current. This caused me to step back and reflect. It was time to do a personal learning inventory, an exercise I highly recommend we all do periodically. With my busy Client and travel schedule, learning and staying current can be a challenge. Here's some of what I find keeps me on the grow:

- Reading material goes everywhere I go, whether on my business trips, or just a trip to the dentist for that 10-minute wait.
- Subscriptions to relevant e-newsletters, magazines, journals, newspapers, and e-zines in the fields of personal, team, and organization effectiveness.
- Buying a large number of books in the fields of personal, team, and organizational development. I read some extensively and scan others for research, experiences, or approaches.
- Morning spiritual reading and meditation.
- Participation in workshops and conventions of the Canadian Association of Professional Speakers and the National Speakers Association.
- Reflections, research, and writing my books, articles,

blog, *The Leader Letter*, and columns.

- Leading interactive workshops, retreats, and keynote presentations with lots of feedback and discussions.
- Client discussions and research to customize my workshops or retreats to that specific organization and/or industry.
- Attending conferences as a speaker where I listen to other speakers and discuss their ideas or experiences one-on-one.
- Working with our CLEMMER Group associates, too, as we learn first-hand what does and doesn't work in bringing about culture change, service or quality improvement, increasing productivity, developing leaders, and so on.
- In my car, I listen to CDs or tapes of conferences or workshops that I'd like to attend if time permits.

Increase Your Emotional Intelligence

"Not only can emotional intelligence be learned, but it also can be retained over the long term....people who successfully change in sustainable ways cycle through the following stages:

- The first discovery: My ideal self — Who do I want to be?

- The second discovery: My real self — Who am I? What are my strengths and gaps?

- The third discovery: My learning agenda — How can I build on my strengths while reducing my gaps?

- The fourth discovery: Experimenting with and practicing new behaviors, thoughts, and feelings to the point of mastery.

- The fifth discovery: Developing supportive and trusting relationships that make change possible.

Ideally, the progression occurs through a discontinuity — a moment of discovery — that provokes not just awareness, but also a sense of urgency."[151]

Daniel Goleman, Richard Boyatzis, and Annie McKee, Primal Leadership: Realizing the Power of Emotional Intelligence

TO KEEP YOU GROWING

Here's where you can find more of my material on the topics covered in this chapter.

www.JimClemmer.com

- A selection of articles on Personal Growth and Continuous Improvement at http://www.jimclemmer.com/growth.
- A selection of my writing and reader discussions on Personal Growth and Continuous Improvement from my **blog** and **monthly newsletter** at http://www.jimclemmer.com/newsletter/?cat=15.

Books

- Chapter One "The Way of the Leader" in *Growing the Distance: Timeless Principles for Personal, Career, and Family Success.*
- "Measuring My Growth," "Signs of Stagnation," "My Learning Style," "Some of My Learning Options," and "Personal Application Ideas" in *Growing the Distance: Self-Study System.*
- Dozens of how-to tips and techniques in the Personal "Pathways and Pitfalls" sections of chapters Thirteen, Fifteen, Eighteen, Nineteen, and Twenty-Four in *Pathways to Performance: A Guide to Transforming Yourself, Your Team, and Your Organization.*

In Conclusion

XVII

Write your own ending. And then begin.

BE AN
ACTION HERO

"I think what we're seeking is an experience of being alive, so that our life experiences on the purely physical plane will have resonance within our own innermost being and reality, so that we actually feel the rapture of being alive. That's what it's all finally about."[152]

Joseph Campbell (1904–1987), American mythologist, writer, and lecturer best known for his work in the fields of comparative mythology and comparative religion

As I was conceiving and wrestling with how to write *Moose on the Table®: A Novel Approach to Communications @ Work*, I was studying Joseph Campbell's 1949 classic book, *The Hero with a Thousand Faces* and watching DVDs of his 1988 PBS television interview series "The Power of Myth" hosted by

Bill Moyers. Originally, I was studying Campbell's work as part of my morning spiritual learning and meditation practice. I was intrigued and inspired by his findings that across all cultures and times, every society's stories, fairy tales, novels, and movies follow a similar "hero's journey." Part of my own writing journey then became creating the story of the fictional hero of *Moose on the Table*®, Pete Leonard, and his journey through fear and avoidance to find the courage to lead.

Campbell outlined 17 common steps, or "legs," of the hero's journey. I group them into three main sections or acts: the call for action, the struggle, and the breakthrough. In the first act, the hero is called to adventure (action) but often refuses the call. Usually a mentor or some other kind of help appears or becomes available. The hero then "crosses the first threshold" and enters or is pushed into the "belly of the whale." This takes the hero into the struggle at the center of the story.

The story's second or main act is the struggle in "the inner-most caves." This is often where fear and courage do battle as the hero faces dangers and numerous tests and trials. As Campbell points out, "The cave you fear to enter holds the treasure you seek." Drama and tension is at its peak here. Will the hero win or will he or she be killed or thrown off course? After ups and downs, wins and losses, there's a breakthrough and the hero succeeds in some way. Key lessons are learned and his or her life has been changed.

In the third or concluding act, our hero returns to his or her previous life ("the ordinary world") with a new perspective, mastery, or learning ("return with the elixir"). The story concludes with a sense of closure or completing the loop, and often a happy ending.

It seemed to me, as I followed this story line for my book, that we are all living in a novel of our own making, with the three acts repeating over and over again. How, I wondered, can we bring that knowledge to our own life learning?

And away we grow.

CHARTING OUR HERO'S JOURNEY

"Everyone is necessarily the hero of his own life story."[53]

John Barth (1930–), professor, award-winning American novelist and short-story writer

Swiss psychiatrist Carl Jung built much of his early to mid-20th century pioneering psychology around the idea of universal archetypes that form models of our core personality types. These include child, hero, mother, wise old man, and trickster or fox. (The Myers-Briggs Type Indicator and other personality models are rooted in this work.) It's fascinating and can be very revealing to contemplate what archetypes or roles we're playing at different points in the various legs of our life's journey. Our levels of courage determine just how deeply we examine our mental frameworks and how we deal with adversity in our life.

Here's a process to map the rest of your life journey, or many of the smaller excursions along the way. You could start by using these steps to reflect on your journey so far, and draw key lessons from them in preparation for your ongoing voyage and the unforeseeable side trips that still lie ahead.

1. What's My Call to Adventure/ Change/Growth?
   • Crisis/Loss (health, death, financial, job, or major market/political shift)?
   • Major event (birth of children, marriage, death of loved ones, restructuring, new job)?

- Big projects (major innovation, merger/acquisition, new home)?
- Personal/spiritual quest?

2. What's my reluctance/resistance to growth/change?
3. What are the rewards of change or costs of failing to change/grow?
4. Who are my mentors/coaches?
5. What are the thresholds (barriers) I need to cross?
6. How will I keep myself above the line as I navigate my growth/changes?
7. How/when will I continually assess progress and refocus?
8. How am I visualizing my happy ending for this change?

Asset or Liability: Who Am I?

I am your constant companion.
I am your greatest asset or heaviest burden.
I will push you up to success or down to disappointment.
I am at your command.

Half the things you do might just as well be turned over to me,
For I can do them quickly, correctly, and profitably.
I am easily managed, just be firm with me.

Those who are great, I have made great.
Those who are failures, I have made failures.
I am not a machine, though I work with the precision of a
machine and the intelligence of a person.

You can run me for profit, or you can run me for ruin.
Show me how you want it done. Educate me. Train me.
Lead me. Reward me.
And I will then...do it automatically.

I am your servant.
Who am I?
I am a habit.

Author Unknown

LEADING HABITS

"The secret of a leader lies in the tests he has faced over the whole course of his life and the habit of action he develops in meeting those tests."

Gail Sheehy (1937–), U.S. journalist and author. Her fifth book, Passages, *has been called "a road map of adult life"*

Our habits make or break us. A habit is a learned behavior causing us to think and act automatically. Many times, we're not aware of the hundreds of tiny and bigger habits we've acquired over our lifetime. Each habit piles on top of another and shapes us into who we are today. These habits create our reality.

Modern psychology's greatest contribution to our health, happiness, and well-being is showing that we're not stuck with any of our habits. It may be neither quick nor easy, but we can change any habit. That's generally done by replacing a bad or unwanted one with a good or desired thought or behavior.

Changing our habitual or automatic and unconscious thinking and actions with more deliberate and carefully chosen perspectives and action is the core theme of *Growing @ the Speed of Change*. As you plan how to change your habits, here's a recap of the key steps we've covered:

- Life is change. It's unpredictable and can be very turbulent.
- Crap happens. The sooner we accept what we can't change, the sooner we can get on with changing what we can.
- There is no objective reality. We're all creating it for ourselves.
- Life is an optical illusion. We change our reality by changing our perception.

- Through our mind-body connection, we can activate our Placebo Effect by our beliefs, expectations, and explanatory style.
- When dealing with change and adversity, we can wallow, follow, or lead.
- The more we wallow below the line in the swamp of fear, the more worry and stress we radiate and magnetize. This can perpetuate a dangerous downward spiral.
- To reduce any negative luck that's being attracted to us, we need to positively charge our energy force field.
- Leadership is an action, not a position. We all need to lead and live above the line.
- We can intelligently choose and change our emotions and dramatically change our lives.
- Three core questions at the center of our being are where we're going, what we believe in, and why we exist.
- Visualization and imagery are key skills in changing our expectations and positively charging our magnetic energy fields.
- The more we align our lives to our core values and strengths, the happier and more successful we'll be.
- Our happiness grows exponentially with increases in our attitude of gratitude.
- We can reprogram our habits by consciously hypnotizing ourselves with affirmations of the characteristics or mindsets we want to strengthen.
- We can reclaim our time and our lives by not letting others "should" on us and not allowing daily urgencies to crowd out what's truly important.
- The more mindful we are of this present moment and observing ourselves, the higher is our enjoyment of the here and now.
- Forgiving people and forgetting past wrongs purges poison from our bodies and empties the sack of stones that sinks us deeper in the swamp.
- Pushing ourselves to have courageous conversations strengthens our leadership muscles and keeps us above the line.
- Upward leadership is as important as leading peers or people at home, in our

community, or anyone reporting to us.

- Asking for help is a sign of strength and confidence that shows we're intelligently using all the resources available to us.
- We increase our influence by increasing our persuasion skills and building networks and collaborations.
- Ongoing personal growth increases our emotional intelligence, leadership skills, and ability to deal with life's constant changes.

Habit-Forming Tips and Techniques

"Cultivate only the habits that you are willing should master you."
Elbert Hubbard (1856–1915), American writer, publisher, artist, and philosopher.

- Draw three columns on a piece of paper with Keep, Stop, and Start at the head of each one. List your main habits under each heading. You might want to get a mentor, close friend, coach, spouse, or someone else who knows you well, whose opinion you trust, and who wants to help you improve, to provide input to your lists.

- You could use one of the last nine chapters outlining "Stepping Up to a New Reality" as your focal point each week. Pick out quotations, Tips and Techniques, or other improvement ideas from each chapter that describe the habit you most want to form. Go to my other development resources referenced at the end of each chapter for even more application ideas on that topic. Keep the key ideas you want to focus on in front of you throughout your day.

- Subscribe to newsletters, blogs, and other electronic feeds to get regular doses of inspiration, instruction, and affirmation.

- Setting personal breakthrough goals that are well beyond your current character, ability, or habits is setting yourself up for failure. That's why crash diets and so many New Year's resolutions are abandoned. Build a series of small wins to celebrate new habits that gather momentum, and you'll find the confidence to keep you growing.

HOPE YOU ENJOYED THE CITY TOUR!

"There's only one corner of the universe you can be certain of improving, and that's your own self."
Aldous Leonard Huxley (1894–1963), English writer

Two of my favorite cities for sightseeing and historical time travel are London and Rome. There are so many layers of history that modern life in both cities is built upon. Rome is especially multilayered. The epicenter of the city — and much of today's Western World — is the ancient Forum of Julius Caesar's day when the Roman Empire was in its prime. Mile marker zero — "all roads lead to Rome" — is here. The Forum with its ancient ruins of government buildings is where the foundations for many of the Western World's social and governing structures were first laid.

Another significant layer laid centuries after the great empire's fall is preserved in Rome's innumerable museums and churches. This time of the European Renaissance provided so much of the art, architecture, engineering, religion, and science that shape modern life today. There are an overwhelming number of sites to see and things to learn in a city like Rome. A broad overview or city tour barely scratches the surface.

Growing @ the Speed of Change is a brief and broad overview of life's choices and how to make those choices more consciously to shape the reality we truly want to create for ourselves during our short time on this earth. Like Rome, I have tried to pull together ancient wisdom, current experiences, and modern research. Like Rome, there's so much more to explore and learn. Some parts of what we've covered may not be relevant or interesting to you. But I hope you've peeked inside a few buildings and enjoyed a few vistas that you'd like to go back to. Spend time in those areas and dig deep. Uncover and answer your call to adventure to keep you moving forward.

Tips and Techniques for Growing Your Way

- Choose your three highest priority areas and put an improvement plan together around them. Schedule time for your improvement as if your career, ability to master change, and happiness depend on it. They do.

- Go deeper into your core topic areas through the other resources referenced at the end of key chapters you want to focus on.

- Look for ways to set improvement goals that build on your strengths and align with your passions and values. You're in this for the long run. Don't sprint. Life is a marathon. Take it step-by-step. You want evolutionary — not revolutionary — change.

- Get input from others on your leading behaviors but ensure that your improvement goals are your own and not imposed on you.

- If your organization has training professionals or a HR department, talk to them to see what personal learning and development options or tools are available to you.

- Start a personal growth or "leading growth" support/study group. Review books, materials, videos, magazine articles, make publicly declared action plans, and report on those at each session. This can be a powerful source of learning from other people's experiences. It's also a great place for you to reflect on your own experiences and articulate your improvement plans.

- Work with your spouse or life partner to map out your shared journey. Set improvement or change goals together around your family, home, community, careers, finances, health and fitness, spirituality, and socializing. Look for opportunities to celebrate individual and joint progress and milestones along the way.

- Focus more on the outcomes or improvements you're looking for than on the exact steps or plans. Those will change as life throws new problems, setbacks, and opportunities at you. Roll with those changes and adjust accordingly.

- Growing the Distance: Self-Study System is an extensive personal growth program with a CD containing my audio track and synchronized slides coaching you through each page of the extensive Growing the Distance: Personal Implementation Guide. You can use the CD thumbnail to jump to those sections you're most interested in developing.

Endnotes

1   *Planning Review,* Marilyn Norris, September/October 1992, Vol. 20 No. 5.

2   Published in *Letters of John Keats,* No. 37, ed. by Frederick Page, 1954.

3   Frederick Fell, Hollywood, FL, 1972, page 12.

4   From *The Globe* of Dec. 10, 1904 cited by Michael Kesterton, *The Globe and Mail,* Friday, December 10, 2004, page A24.

5   *The Peter Pyramid,* Laurence J. Peter, William Morrow and Company, New York, 1986, page 176.

6   "When did our lives go global? Try 300 AD" by Doug Saunders, *The Globe and Mail,* August 28, 2004, page F3.

7   *The Essential Drucker,* Harper Business, New York, 2001, page 347. Reprinted by permission of HarperCollins Publishers, Inc., from THE ESSENTIAL DRUCKER, Peter Drucker. Copyright © 2001 by Peter F. Drucker. The Best of Sixty Years of Peter Drucker's Essential Writings on Management. For additional territory contact: Joan Drucker Winstein, co-trustee of the Drucker Literary Trust, 424 North Linden Avenue, Oak Park, IL, 60302 708 383 0403, pfd1909@yahoo.com. Territory Granted: United States, ITS DEP., Canada, Philippine Islands, Open Market.

8   "When did our lives go global? Try 300 AD" by Doug Saunders, *The Globe and Mail,* August 28, 2004, page F3.

9   *Built to Change: How to Achieve Sustained Organizational Effectiveness,* Edward E. Lawler III and Christopher G. Worley, Jossey-Bass, 2006, San Francisco, CA, page 1. Reprinted with permission of John Wiley & Sons, Inc.

10 *The New Road to the Top,* Peter Cappelli and Monika Hamori, *Harvard Business Review,* January 2005, page 26.

11 *The Quest for Resilience,* Gary Hamel and Liisa Välikangas, *Harvard Business Review,* September 2003, page 52.

12 *The Fortune Sellers: The Big Business of Buying and Selling Predictions,* William Sherden, John Wiley & Sons, New York, 1998, page iii. Reprinted with permission of John Wiley & Sons, Inc.

13 October 5, 2008. Posted at www.boston.com, (http://www.boston.com/bostonglobe/ideas/articles/2008/10/05/a_talk_with_philip_tetlock).

14 January 30, 2006. Posted at http://money.cnn.com/magazines/fortune/fortune_archive/2006/02/06/8367977/index.htm.

15 December 5, 2005. Posted at www.newyorker.com, (http://www.newyorker.com/archive/2005/12/05/051205crbo_books1?currentPage=1).

16 *The Prophets of Profit,* Steven Theobald reporting on *The Toronto Star's* analysis of 20 years of mostly inaccurate annual forecasts, November 24, 2002.

17 *The Fortune Sellers: The Big Business of Buying and Selling Predictions,* William Sherden, John Wiley & Sons, New York, 1998, pages 61, 62, 65, and 78. Reprinted with permission of John Wiley & Sons, Inc.

18 American Media Inc., Boca Raton, FL, 2004, page 14.

19 "Buddhists accept insecurity as a way of life," *Toronto Star,* January 11, 2003.

20 *The Art of Happiness: A Handbook for Living*, His Holiness the Dalai Lama and Howard C. Cutler, M.D., Riverhead Books, New York, 1998, page 191.

21 *Built to Change: How to Achieve Sustained Organizational Effectiveness*, Edward E. Lawler III and Christopher G. Worley, Jossey-Bass, 2006, San Francisco, CA, pages 21 and 22. Reprinted with permission of John Wiley & Sons, Inc.

22 *The Soul of Man Under Socialism,* in *Fortnightly Review* (London, February 1891; reprinted 1895).

23 Quoted in *Making a Life Making a Living: Reclaiming your Purpose and Passion in Business and in Life*, Mark Alboin, Warner Books, New York, 2000, page 198.

24 *Becoming Human,* Jean Vanier, Anansi Press, Don Mills, ON, 1998, page 13.

25 *The Dancing Wu Li Masters: An Overview of the New Physics*, Gary Zukav, Bantam Books, 1979, New York, page 310.

26 http://wordnetweb.princeton.edu/perl/webwn?o2=&o0=1&o7=&o5=&o1=1&o6=&o4=&o3=&s=reality &i=0&h=0000#c.

27 http://www.answers.com/topic/quote-4?subject=Reality&s2=Reality.

28 http://www.answers.com/topic/quote-4?subject=Reality&s2=Reality.

29 http://www.answers.com/topic/quote-4?subject=Reality&s2=Reality.

30 *What the Bleep Do We Know*, William Arntz, Betsy Chasse, and Mark Vicente, Health Communications, Deerfield Beach, FL, 2005, page 53. Reprinted with permission of Health Communications, Inc.

31 *What the Bleep Do We Know*, William Arntz, Betsy Chasse, and Mark Vicente, Health Communications, Deerfield Beach, FL, 2005, page 36. Reprinted with permission of Health Communications, Inc.

32 *Recovering the Soul: A Scientific and Spiritual Search*, Larry Dossey, Bantam, New York, 1989, page 93.

33 Suzie Daggett interview posted at http://www.dramitgoswami.com/Quantum_Questions.asp.

34 *What the Bleep Do We Know: Discovering the Endless Possibilities for Altering Your Everyday Reality,* William Arntz, Betsy Chasse, and Mark Vicente, Health Communications, Deerfield Beach, FL, 2005, pages 36 and 56. Reprinted with permission of Health Communications, Inc.

35 In Nina L. Diamond, Voices of Truth (2000), 324. at www.todayinsci.com/ QuotationsCategories/S_Cat/StringTheory-Quotations.htm.

36 http://www.brainyquote.com/quotes/authors/e/edward_witten.html.

37 *Why is Life?,* Dennis Gaumond, Aten Publishing, Guelph, ON, 2004, page 99.

38 *Why is Life?,* Dennis Gaumond, Aten Publishing, Guelph, ON, 2004, page 98.

39 *The Hidden Messages in Water*, Masaru Emoto, Beyond Words, Hillsboro, OR, 2004, pages 43 and 44.

40 http://www.hado.net/hado/index.php.

41 *The Hidden Messages in Water*, Masaru Emoto, Beyond Words, Hillsboro, OR, 2004, pages 43 and 44.

42 *Meaning, Medicine and the 'Placebo Effect,'* Daniel Moerman, Cambridge University Press, Cambridge, UK, 2002, page 67. Printed with permission of Cambridge University Press.

43 *The Inside Edge: High Performance Through Mental Fitness*, Peter Jensen, Performance Coaching, Rockwood, ON, 1994, page 30.

44 *What the Bleep Do We Know!?*, William Arntz, Betsy Chasse, and Mark Vicente, Health Communications, Deerfield Beach, FL, 2005, page 49. Reprinted with permission of Health Communications, Inc.

45 Source: Jastrow, J. (1899). The mind's eye. *Popular Science Monthly*, 54, 299-312 from http://en.wikipedia.org/wiki/File:Duck-Rabbit_illusion.jpg.

46 http://www.bartleby.com/61/62/P0216200.html.

47 http://www.bartleby.com/61/21/00102100.html.

48 *Authentic Happiness: Using the New Positive Psychology to Realize Your Potential for Lasting Fulfillment*, Martin Seligman, Free Press, New York, 2002, page 24. Reprinted with the permission of The Free Press, a Division of Simon & Schuster, Inc. from AUTHENTIC HAPPINESS: Using the New Positive Psychology to Realize Your Potential for Lasting Fulfillment by Martin E. Seligman. Copyright © 2002 by Martin Seligman. All rights reserved.

49 *Authentic Happiness: Using the New Positive Psychology to Realize Your Potential for Lasting Fulfillment*, Martin Seligman, Free Press, New York, 2002, page 83. Reprinted with the permission of The Free Press, a Division of Simon & Schuster, Inc. from AUTHENTIC HAPPINESS: Using the New Positive Psychology to Realize Your Potential for Lasting Fulfillment by Martin E. Seligman. Copyright © 2002 by Martin Seligman. All rights reserved.

50 October 1, 1952, http://www.bartleby.com/63/51/5151.html.

51 *The EQ Edge. Emotional Intelligence and Your Success*, Steven J. Stein and Howard E. Book, Stoddart Publishing, Toronto, 2000, page 212.

52 "Brain Check," *Newsweek*, Herbert Benson (Mind/Body Medical Institute Associate Professor of Medicine at Harvard Medical School), Julie Corliss (medical writer at Harvard Medical School), and Geoffrey Cowley (*Newsweek's* health editor) September 27, 2004.

53 *Meaning, Medicine and the 'Placebo Effect,'* Daniel Moerman, Cambridge University Press, Cambridge, UK, 2002, page 106. Reprinted with permission of Cambridge University Press.

54 *Recovering the Soul: A Scientific and Spiritual Search*, Larry Dossey, Bantam, New York, 1989, page 264.

55 *Molecules of Emotion,* Candace Pert, Scribner, New York, 1997, page 273.

56 "Sports Doping's Effect May Be in the Mind," *HealthDay,* June 17, 2008.

57 *Man's Search for Meaning*, Viktor Emil Frankl, Washington Square Press, New York, 1985, page 87.

58 *Getting Things Done When You Are Not in Charge*, Geoffrey M. Bellman, Berrett-Koehler, San Francisco, 2001, pages 102 and103. Reprinted with permission of Berrett-Koehler Publishers Inc., All rights reserved. www.bkconnection.com.

59 *Meaning, Medicine and the 'Placebo Effect,'* Daniel Moerman, Cambridge University Press, Cambridge, UK, 2002, page 114. Reprinted with permission of Cambridge University Press.

60 *Primal Leadership: The Hidden Driver of Great Performance*, Daniel Goleman, Richard Boyatzis, and Annie McKee, *Harvard Business Review*, December, 2001, page 46. Reprinted with permission of *Harvard Business Review*.

61 *Authentic Happiness: Using the New Positive Psychology to Realize Your Potential for Lasting Fulfillment*, Martin Seligman, Free Press, New York, 2002, page 27.

Reprinted with the permission of The Free Press, a Division of Simon & Shuster, Inc. from AUTHENTIC HAPPINESS: Using the New Positive Psychology to Realize Your Potential for Lasting Fulfillment by Martin E. Seligman. Copyright © 2002 by Martin Seligman. All rights reserved.

62 *The Globe and Mail*, September 9, 2002, page A14.

63 "It Pays to Be Optimistic," Jennifer Robison, *Gallup Management Journal*, August 9, 2007.

64 *Authentic Happiness: Using the New Positive Psychology to Realize Your Potential for Lasting Fulfillment,* Martin Seligman, Free Press, New York, 2002, page 202. Reprinted with the permission of The Free Press, a Division of Simon & Shuster, Inc. from AUTHENTIC HAPPINESS: Using the New Positive Psychology to Realize Your Potential for Lasting Fulfillment by Martin E. Seligman. Copyright © 2002 by Martin Seligman. All rights reserved.

65 *The Globe and Mail*, September 9, 2002, page A14.

66 *Authentic Happiness: Using the New Positive Psychology to Realize Your Potential for Lasting Fulfillment*, Martin Seligman, Free Press, New York, 2002, page 10. Reprinted with the permission of The Free Press, a Division of Simon & Shuster, Inc., from AUTHENTIC HAPPINESS: Using the New Positive Psychology to Realize Your Potential for Lasting Fulfillment by Martin E. Seligman. Copyright © 2002 by Martin Seligman. All rights reserved.

67 "Optimism & the Prevention of Heart Attack," Martin Seligman, *Reflective Happiness* newsletter, July 2005, Volume 1, N. 7.

68 *The Inside Edge: High Performance Through Mental Fitness*, Peter Jensen, Performance Coaching, Rockwood, ON, 1994, pages 4 and 5.

69 Alfred A. Knopf, New York, 1990.

70 *Reflective Happiness* newsletter, Sent: Tuesday, August 8, 2006.

71 *Authentic Happiness: Using the New Positive Psychology to Realize Your Potential for Lasting Fulfillment*, Martin Seligman, Free Press, New York, 2002, page 24. Reprinted with the permission of The Free Press, a Division of Simon & Shuster, Inc. from AUTHENTIC HAPPINESS: Using the New Positive Psychology to Realize Your Potential for Lasting Fulfillment by Martin E. Seligman. Copyright © 2002 by Martin Seligman. All rights reserved.

72 *Authentic Happiness: Using the New Positive Psychology to Realize Your Potential for Lasting Fulfillment*, Martin Seligman, Free Press, New York, 2002, page 28. Reprinted with the permission of The Free Press, a Division of Simon & Shuster, Inc. from AUTHENTIC HAPPINESS: Using the New Positive Psychology to Realize Your Potential for Lasting Fulfillment by Martin E. Seligman. Copyright © 2002 by Martin Seligman. All rights reserved.

73 http://www.ppc.sas.upenn.edu.

74 *The Luck Factor: Change Your Luck and Change Your Life*, Richard Wiseman, Century, London, 2002, pages 108 and 109. Reprinted by permission of The Random House Group Ltd.

75 *The Luck Factor: Change Your Luck and Change Your Life*, Richard Wiseman, Century, London, 2002, pages 107 and 108. Reprinted by permission of The Random House Group Ltd.

76 *The Luck Factor: Change Your Luck and Change Your Life*, Richard Wiseman, Century, London, 2002, page 172. Reprinted by permission of The Random House Group Ltd.

77 "Who Says Quitters Never Win?" Wray Herbert, *Newsweek* Web Exclusive, September 27, 2007.

78 http://thinkexist.com/quotes/warren_g._bennis.

79 "How Resilience Works," Diane L. Coutu, *Harvard Business Review*, May 2002, page 47. Reprinted with permission of *Harvard Business Review*.

80 "The Hidden Side of Happiness," Kathleen McGowan, *Psychology Today*, March/April 2006, Document ID: 3994.

81 "How Resilience Works," Diane L. Coutu, *Harvard Business Review*, May 2002, pages 48, 50, and 55. Reprinted with permission of *Harvard Business Review*.

82 *Good to Great*, Jim Collins, Harper Business, New York, 2001, page 82.

83 *Mindfulness*, 1989, pages 53 and 54 at http://timpanogos.wordpress.com/2007/11/14/quote-of-the-moment-ellen-langer-on-learned-helplessness.

84 Wendin Nah, May 21, 2008, posted at http://www.scienceray.com/Biology/Marine-Biology/What-is-the-Pike-Syndrome.127739.

85 "Rotten to the core: How workplace 'bad apples' spoil barrels of good employees," Nancy Gardner, February 12, 2007, *University of Washington News*, posted at http://uwnews.org/article.asp?articleID=30464.

86 "Defending Yourself Against Energy Vampires," Interview by Karen Elmhirst, November 8, 2004, posted at http://www.hr.com//SITEFORUM;jsessionid= B73E5C4EEF872A57FC77CCAA16BDF075?t=/CustomCode/webcasts/videoContainer&i=1116423256281&l =0&e=UTF-8&videoLink=http://media.hr.com/webinarslibrary/TLDrJudith Orloff11080416548454544.swf.

87 "SARS and the Fear Factor," *Maclean's*, April 21, 2003.

88 *Life of Pi*, Yann Martel, Random House, Toronto, 2001, pages 178 and 179.

89 "The Making of an Expert," K. Anders Ericsson, Michael J. Prietula, and Edward T. Cokely, July-August 2007, page 116.

90 "Why Talent is Overrated," *Fortune*, October 21, 2008.

91 "Social Studies: A Daily Miscellany of Information," Michael Kesterton, *The Globe and Mail*, May 5, 2003, page A18. Quoted from Richard Stengel in *Time* magazine.

92 "Overloaded Circuits: Why Smart People Underperform," *Harvard Business Review*, January 2005, pages 55 and 56.

93 "You've got too much mail," Katherine Maclem, *Maclean's*, January 25, 2006.

94 "Is Silence Killing Your Company?" Leslie Perlow and Stephanie Williams, *Harvard Business Review*, Excerpted from the Executive Summary for the article in May 2003, pages 52 to 58.

95 "The Recession Lovers' Club," Rob Norton, *Fortune*, April 1, 2002, page 42.

96 Templeton Foundation Press, Philadelphia, 1997, page 2.

97 "Don't worry, be happy ... or not," Lynda Hurst, *Toronto Star*, April 1, 2007.

98 Condensed from *The Kreutzer Sonata and Other Short Stories*, Leo Tolstoy, Dover Publications, New York, 1993, posted at http://www.katinkahesselink.net/other/tolstoy.html.

99 *The Extraordinary Leader: Turning Good Managers Into Great Leaders*, Jack H. Zenger and Joseph Folkman, McGraw-Hill, New York, 2002, page 160.

100 http://aesopfables.com/cgi/aesop1.cgi?sel&TheBeeandJupiter.

101 *Getting Things Done When You Are Not in Charge,* Geoffrey M. Bellman, Berrett-Koehler, San Francisco, 2001, page 1. Reprinted with permission of Berrett-Koehler Publishers, Inc., All rights reserved. www.bkconnection.com.

102 "Why Everyone in an Enterprise Can – and Should – Be a Leader," December 23, 2003 in Knowledge@Wharton at http://knowledge.wharton.upenn.edu/article.cfm?articleid=893.

103 December 23, 2003 in Knowledge@Wharton at http://knowledge.wharton.upenn.edu/article.cfm?articleid=893.

104 *Recovering the Soul: A Scientific and Spiritual Search,* Dr. Larry Dossey, Bantam, New York, 1989, page 63.

105 *Primal Leadership: Realizing the Power of Emotional Intelligence,* Daniel Goleman, Richard Boyatzis, and Annie McKee, Harvard Business School Press, Boston, MA, 2002, page 5.

106 *Executive EQ: Emotional Intelligence in Leadership and Organizations,* Robert K. Cooper and Aymen Sawaf, Penguin Putnam, New York, 1997, page xxxi.

107 *Working with Emotional Intelligence,* Daniel Goleman, Bantam Books, New York, 1998, page 19.

108 *Primal Leadership: Realizing the Power of Emotional Intelligence,* Daniel Goleman, Richard Boyatzis, and Annie McKee, Harvard Business School Press, Boston, MA, 2002, page 251.

109 "The Business Case for Emotional Intelligence," Cary Cherniss, Rutgers University, Prepared for the Consortium for Research on Emotional Intelligence in Organizations and posted at http://www.eiconsortium.org/reports/business_case_for_ei.html

110 *Working with Emotional Intelligence,* Daniel Goleman, Bantam Books, New York, 1998, page 29.

111 *Working with Emotional Intelligence,* Daniel Goleman, Bantam Books, New York, 1998, page 187.

112 www.Wikipedia.org.

113 *Harvard Business Review,* February 2007, page 27.

114 "The Harder They Fall," *Harvard Business Review,* October 2003, page 66.

115 *The Tao of Leadership: Lao Tzu's Tao Te Ching Adapted for a New Age,* John Heider, Bantam, New York, 1986, page 51.

116 *Harvard Business Review,* September 2008, page 80.

117 "Why Emotional Intelligence Matters," Martha Brant interview of Travis Bradberry, *Newsweek,* June 14, 2005.

118 "Leading by Feel," *Harvard Business Review,* January 2004, page 30. Reprinted with permission of *Harvard Business Review.*

119 "Leading by Feel," *Harvard Business Review,* January 2004, page 32. Reprinted with permission of *Harvard Business Review.*

120 "Leading by Feel," *Harvard Business Review,* January 2004, page 35. Reprinted with permission of *Harvard Business Review.*

121 *The Positive Power of Negative Thinking: Using Defensive Pessimism to Harness Anxiety and Perform at Your Peak,* Julie Norem, Basic Books, Cambridge, MA, 2002, pages 2 and 3.

122 *Getting Things Done When You Are Not in Charge,* Geoffrey Bellman, Berrett-Koehler, San Francisco, 2001, page 2. Reprinted with permission of Berrett-Koehler Publishers, Inc., All rights reserved. www.bkconnection.com.

123 "The next great curse: self-inflicted ADD at work," Wallace Immen, *The Globe and Mail,* July 7, 2006.

124 *The Luck Factor: Change Your Luck and Change your Life,* Richard Wiseman, Century, London, 2002, page 134.

125 The Reilly & Lee Co., Chicago, 1916.

126 From "The Edinburgh Lectures on Mental Science" delivered at Queens Gate in Edinburgh, Scotland in 1904 posted at http://thomastroward.wwwhubs.com/teloms5.htm.

127 The Hidden Power and Other Papers Upon Mental Science, Robert M. McBride & Company, New York, 1921.

128 Posted at http://www.cmbm.org/downloads/What_is_Mind_Body_Medicine.pdf.

129 *The Five Stages of the Soul: Charting the Spiritual Passages That Shape Our Lives,* Harry Moody and David Carroll, Doubleday, New York, 1997, page 50.

130 *Working with Emotional Intelligence,* Daniel Goleman, Bantam Books, New York, 1998, page 58.

131 *Authentic Happiness: Using the New Positive Psychology to Realize Your Potential for Lasting Fulfillment,* Martin Seligman, Free Press, New York, 2002, page xiii. Reprinted with the permission of The Free Press, a Division of Simon & Shuster, Inc. from AUTHENTIC HAPPINESS: Using the New Positive Psychology to Realize Your Potential for Lasting Fulfillment by Martin E. Seligman. Copyright © 2002 by Martin Seligman. All rights reserved.

132 www.wmitchell.com.

133 *Self-Mastery Through Conscious Autosuggestion,* Emile Coué, American Library Service Publishers, New York, 1922.

134 *Authentic Happiness: Using the New Positive Psychology to Realize Your Potential for Lasting Fulfillment,* Martin Seligman, Free Press, New York, 2002, page 93. Reprinted with the permission of The Free Press, a Division of Simon & Shuster, Inc. from AUTHENTIC HAPPINESS: Using the New Positive Psychology to Realize Your Potential for Lasting Fulfillment by Martin E. Seligman. Copyright © 2002 by Martin Seligman. All rights reserved.

135 *Crazy Busy: Overstretched, Overbooked, and About To Snap,* Edward M. Hallowell, Ballantine Books, New York, 2006, page 10.

136 "Beware the Busy Manager," Heike Bruch and Sumantra Ghoshal, *Harvard Business Review,* February 2002, pages 64, 67, and 68.

137 "Mastering Your Own Mind," Katherine Ellison, *Psychology Today* magazine, September/October 2006.

138 *The Power of Now,* Eckhart Tolle, New World Library, 2004, Novota, CA, pages 49, 58, 64, and 65.

139 "Let Thrift Be Your Ruling Habit," posted at http://www.foundationsmag.com/thrift.html.

140 *Gardens from the Sand: A Story About Looking for Answers and Finding Miracles,* Dan Cavicchio, Harper Collins, New York, 1994, page 60.

141 *The Globe and Mail,* Wednesday, March 5, 2003, page A18.

142 *Leading Up: How to Lead Your Boss so You Both Win,* Michael Useem, Random House, New York, 2001, page 6.

143 "Survey Shows 48% Would Fire Their Boss," Posted: 6/15/2004 8:00:00 AM at http://www.badbossology.com/i4784-c139.

144 "Telling the boss from hell (politely and tactfully) where to go," Marjo Johne, *The Globe and Mail*, March 14, 2008.

145 *Tempered Radicals: How People Use Difference to Inspire Change at Work*, Debra E. Meyerson, Harvard Business School Press, Boston, MA, 2001, pages 166 and 171.

146 *Social Intelligence: The New Science of Human Relationships*, Daniel Goleman, Bantam Books, New York, 2006, quote is from front cover flap.

147 "The Necessary Art of Persuasion," Jay Conger, *Harvard Business Review*, May-June 1998, page 87.

148 *Working with Emotional Intelligence*, Daniel Goleman, Bantam Books, New York, 1998, page 173.

149 *Tempered Radicals: How People Use Difference to Inspire Change at Work*, Debra E. Meyerson, Harvard Business School Press, Boston, MA, 2001, pages 40, 41, and 55.

150 Excerpted from The Project Gutenberg Etext at http://www.gutenberg.org/dirs/etext03/mntkh10.txt.

151 *Primal Leadership: Realizing the Power of Emotional Intelligence*, Daniel Goleman, Richard Boyatzis, and Annie McKee, Harvard Business School Press, Boston, MA, 2002, pages 111 and 112.

152 *Joseph Campbell and The Power of Myth with Bill Moyers*, PBS television series, Mystic Fire Video (2001) Episode 2, Chapter 4.

153 *The End of the Road*, John Barth, Bantam Books, 1978, page 88.

Index

Get Jim's Personal Coaching with
Growing the Distance: Self-Study System

Now you can have Jim as your personal coach. Or you can bring him into your organization to coach everyone. With the *Growing the Distance: Self-Study System*, he will coach you or others throughout your organization, on how to apply the Timeless Leadership Principles that has made *Growing the Distance* so popular with over 100,000 readers worldwide.

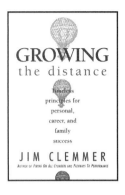

The *Growing the Distance: Self-Study System* features an audio track and synchronized slides with Jim coaching you through each page of the *Growing the Distance*: *Personal Implementation Guide*. You are in complete control. You can run the program in the order and process that it's designed. Or you can pause wherever you want, skip ahead, return to sections, or skim through the program and pluck out those sections most relevant and useful to you. With a handy thumbnail outline, you can click on any slide and hear its corresponding audio. You get the benefit of Jim's extensive experience and coaching help customized to your own personal needs and developmental interests.

Growing the Distance: Timeless Principles for Personal, Career, and Family Success pioneered the magazine style format used in *The Leader's Digest* and *Growing @ the Speed of Change*. The *Growing the Distance* book, *Personal Implementation Guide*, and *Self-Study System* are all built around The CLEMMER Group's Timeless Leadership Principles:

- *Focus and Context: The Core of My Being*
- *Responsibility for Choices: If It's to Be, It's Up to Me*
- *Authenticity: Getting Real*
- *Passion and Commitment: Beyond Near-Life Experiences*
- *Spirit and Meaning: With All My Heart and Soul*
- *Growing and Developing: From Phase of Life to Way of Life*
- *Mobilizing and Energizing: Putting Emotions in Motion*

To view sample excerpts, reviews, and deep discounts visit our online Book Store at www.JimClemmer.com

Use *Growing @ the Speed of Change* as a Tool for Team or Organizational Change

When everyone in your organization accepts, expects, and acknowledges constant change, you'll see immediate benefits

Change isn't news. But the dramatically accelerating pace of organizational change is. People feel inundated, overwhelmed, and stressed. Adaptive organizations provide inspiration and practical tools to everyone in order to help deal with the rapid pace of change and uncertainty.

Turbulent times have created a tsunami of fear, frustration, and uncertainty. When these negative forces flood through the workplace, they often wash away morale and motivation. This can create "change fatigue" as organizations deal with:

- Continuous changes in leadership, direction, and priorities
- Constant reorganizing and restructuring
- Relentless pressure to do more with less
- Ever increasing customer demands
- Accelerating cycles of new technologies, methods, and approaches
- An endless stream of new processes and procedures
- Unpredictable markets, economies, and public mood swings
- A rapidly shifting workforce with a new generation of employees bringing different expectations
- Perpetual reshaping of major sectors through mergers, acquisitions or bankruptcies
- Unceasing pressure to continuously innovate and grow in response to global competition

It's impossible to predict where all this change is taking us. But one thing is certain – the pace of change is going to keep accelerating. And to thrive in turbulent times, organizations must change perceptions and behaviors to change results.

Replace fear and cynicism with refocused perspective and inspired action

With so many factors beyond the control of supervisors, managers and executives, it's easy to forget the one thing we do control is our reaction to change. *Growing @ the Speed of Change* will **help everyone in your organization accept, and adapt to a culture of constant change.**

Today everyone must be a leader

A key message in *Growing @ the Speed of Change* is **leadership is an action, not a position.** When developed across an organization, leader behavior reverses the draining forces of change fatigue, de-motivation, and slipping morale. *Growing @ the Speed of Change* is **written, and priced, for broad distribution** to front line, as well as, supervisory and management staff who need to accept change, and adapt to the challenges and opportunities it brings.

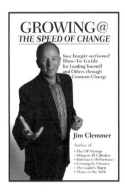

Now, more than ever, we need leaders at all levels and all roles. This book develops organization-wide leadership behaviors, and fosters a new appreciation for the opportunities constant change brings.

Bring order to chaotic change

Living in fear of the next change or wallowing in frustration doesn't foster creativity, productivity, or focus on the immediate task at hand. *Growing @ the Speed of Change* will:

- Help staff at all levels deal with change, uncertainty, and turbulence
- Provide practical approaches to improve morale, increase engagement, and boost energy
- Foster personal growth and development within an engaging and highly accessible book – written for people who often don't read this type of material
- Increase shared leadership throughout your entire organization
- Reinforce organizational values and culture with key messages and approaches that encourage positivity, teamwork and a "can-do" spirit
- Strengthen buy in and personal commitment to organizational change and improvement efforts
- Supplement learning and development programs with an inspir-*actional* resource providing practical tips and techniques to capitalize on constant change

Go to www.JimClemmer.com/GSC for *deep discounts* that start at just 5 books

Grow Stronger Leaders with *The Leader's Digest* and *Practical Application Planner*

Based on the overwhelmingly positive feedback for his previous bestseller, *Growing the Distance*, Jim Clemmer wrote *The Leader's Digest* using the same "leadership wheel" framework. By popular demand, he continues with the unique magazine style format, interweaving pithy quotations, anecdotes, and insightful commentary.

Written for supervisors, managers, and executives, *The Leader's Digest* is built around The CLEMMER Group's Timeless Leadership Principles:

- *Focus and Context: Points of Origin*
- *Responsibility for Choices: From Victim to Victor*
- *Authenticity: Let's Get Real*
- *Passion and Commitment: All Fired Up*
- *Spirit and Meaning: Matters of the Heart*
- *Growing and Developing: All That We Can Be*
- *Mobilizing and Energizing: Go Team, Go*

Develop your Leadership Team with the *Practical Application Planner*

The *Practical Application Planner* moves management teams from being inspired by *The Leader's Digest* to applying its Timeless Leadership Principles. This needs to be an ongoing process, not just a "sheep dip" event (*one-size-fits-all* training that isn't always immediately applicable). Successful team development and organizational leadership comes from many small steps over a long period of time.

Inspiring and jam-packed with *practical* application ideas, *The Leader's Digest: Practical Application Planner* is a cost-effective way to enrich leadership development initiatives:

- Reinforce new or existing development programs
- Shift organizational culture toward stronger people leadership
- Bond management teams with a common set of principles
- Provide compelling evidence that hard results come from "soft skills"
- Bolster emotional intelligence throughout leadership staff

To view sample excerpts, reviews, and deep discounts visit our online Book Store at www.JimClemmer.com